To our parents,
Phil and Mary, Joe and Elizabeth,
who reached fifty years of marriage
as we reached twenty-five.
Thank you
for showing us the way.

Contents

She Said, He Said

Ann

Michael, we should talk about all the lessons we learned in twenty-five years of marriage, and how God has been with us every step of the way.

Mike

Annie, nobody wants to hear all that.

Falling in Love
This wasn't on my agenda.

Ann

Michael and I met at a fraternity costume party. I was dressed as "Aphrodite, goddess of love," a choice which legitimized my tiny white toga, a skating costume on loan from a friend. Michael wore head-to-toe black and said he was "Zorro," pointing to his broad-brimmed hat and rapier.

It was Halloween weekend at the University of Michigan. Michael had flown in from New York that Friday on a road trip to visit his identical twin, Chris, a sophomore at Michigan. They hadn't seen each other in two months. But after Michael and I met,

Michael postponed his return flight, scuttled the brother bonding time, and took me out to dinner.

Michael returned the next month, escorting me to a sorority barn dance where we drank spiked cider and laughed through attempts at square dancing, in between the asthma attacks Michael sustained from the hay bales.

Michael made me laugh. I liked him. But he lived a thousand miles away. He admitted he had a girlfriend back home, and I was dating other people, too. Eventually, the spark between us would fade, returning us to our separate lives a half-continent apart.

Then something happened that fanned the spark to a flame: a blood vessel ruptured inside my brain.

I was home for two weeks of Christmas break, when an explosion of pain in my head sent me to the hospital, my mother acting as emergency ambulance driver. We found out I'd had an AVM bleed in my brain. AVM stands for "arteriovenous malformation" – a congenital malformed blood vessel. We learned that the AVM could bleed again at any time - and that a bleed can be fatal. I lay half-conscious in the hospital for two weeks. I would not return to school for months.

I came home to wait in my darkened bedroom for the pain to subside, for life to resume some normalcy. Michael called many times. I clung to his voice as a lifeline. I was lonely and scared. The only cure for my AVM was a high-risk surgery. According to the neurosurgeons, the operation carried a fifty percent chance of paralysis and a ten percent chance of death.

Michael came to see me two months later during his spring break. It was a magical week, each day like a stolen treasure, sparkling with happiness and hope.

We fell in love.

I was scheduled for surgery two weeks later. When we said goodbye, we didn't know if it would be the last time. But a measured second opinion and a week of agonizing prayer swung my parents and me against the neurosurgery. I would entrust my health not to the surgeons, but to the Great Physician who watches over all of us. I returned to my classes at Michigan that summer, and Michael's and my long distance relationship blossomed.

The next year offered plenty of opportunities to reconsider.

I was a small town girl from Michigan, the oldest of four daughters in a tradition-bound family. My sisters and I went to church with our parents every Sunday and sat down together each day for breakfast and for dinner, a meat-and-potatoes affair with the occasional canned Chicken Chow Mein offering a sprinkle of international variety.

I noticed that Michael's upbringing presented some contrasts to mine. Michael and Chris were Long Island boys, their parents easy-going, fun-loving types who liked to live large and laugh. Phil was Italian, their mother Mary was Chinese, and although they celebrated Christmas, the family seemed to view church less as a place of worship and more as a catering venue for weddings and funerals.

Yet Michael and I felt a kinship, a shared purpose that pushed aside the differences between our families. Our conversations were about Life and God and Purpose. I felt in my heart we belonged together, and so did he. After college graduation we married.

We settled in Atlanta. We called it "our city," finding there the urban pace of New York united with the warmth and religious tradition of the Midwest. Over the next ten years, we weathered Michael's medical training and the birth of our two boys. Michael accepted a position as an OB/GYN in a small-town practice, and we left for the wide green suburbs north of Atlanta.

We were ready for a new set of adventures.

Tyler was three and Joseph was a newborn. As we settled into parenting and our new life, Michael began to write at night and on the weekends, sifting through his experiences in learning to be a doctor at Atlanta's Grady Hospital; he was driven to share what he had learned from serving the city's poorest and sickest patients - stories of faith, hope, and miracles.

Michael's first published piece appeared in a local magazine called *The Townelaker*. Within a few years his monthly articles had spread to a half-dozen magazines, winning a couple of state-wide awards and culminating in the publication of his first book, *The Eyes Don't See*, a collection of stories about health and faith. As the boys grew older, raising a family put new pressures on Michael's and my relationship, and tales of our struggles began to figure prominently. It is these stories which make up this second book about family.

The most important relationships in our lives are often the most difficult. Michael's stories show how God gently led us through the lessons of marriage and family; Michael shares the problems and conclusions of a husband and father.

But these were not always the same as mine. A man and a woman, a surgeon and an artist, a New Yorker and a Midwest girl, experience marriage and family in very different ways.

So for the many readers who have asked over the years, "What did Ann say about *that?*" – we've included my side, too.

Mike

It was her pretty smile and skimpy Halloween outfit that first attracted me like a moth to a flame. I was in my second year at Wesleyan University. It was an unhappy time of my life. I had chosen the college because it was reputed to have an excellent program for premedical students. Wesleyan was also known for its "diversity." That was fine with me. As a punk kid from Long Island, I pictured diversity as blondes, brunettes, and redheads.

Not communists, homosexuals, and women who didn't shave under their arms.

In the fall of my sophomore year, I visited my twin brother, Chris, at the University of Michigan. Now *this* was what I had imagined college would be like! Chris and I hung out with his fraternity brothers at a football game. We drank beer. Later that night, we went to a Halloween party on campus where I met my future wife.

I can honestly say I had never before met anyone like Ann.

Ann was a Christian.

She was a Republican.

And she was a Virgin.

You didn't have many of those at Wesleyan - not that I had been looking. I had a serious girlfriend back in New York who was less a virgin and more a Victoria's Secret model nymphomaniac. This was another reason I was unhappy at Wesleyan. I zoomed off campus every chance I could to be with her.

Two months later, Ann was in a hospital with a life-threatening bleed in her brain. I found out while I was home in New York for Christmas break. I woke in the middle of the night thinking about her. I drove to a Long Island beach to settle my thoughts. I walked for miles in the dark, listening to the sounds of waves crashing, looking at the stars, and wondering why I was there.

Finally, I prayed.

God answered me. It wasn't a booming voice from the sky. But there was a knowingness that came over my heart. I wasn't sure what would happen to Ann, but I knew what all this meant.

If Ann died, I would celebrate the short time I had known her with an increased spiritual awareness of the fragility of life, dedicating myself to becoming the person that God meant me to become.

And if Ann lived, I would realize that God was sending me a signal flare!

This book is a celebration of the twenty-five

years of our marriage. Ann has been the greatest blessing in my life. I hardly deserve her as my wife. That's not to say she isn't sometimes an annoying human being to be around. But I am worse by far. I am grateful she has tolerated me all these years.

1

Family Culture Clash

Ann *Michael, we should capitalize*
on our different strengths
to come up with
the best possible parenting strategy.

Mike Hey, lighten up, sweetie.
Sometimes
you just have to wing it.

Mothering

It's a lot more work than fathering.

Ann

When the boys were little, Michael and I began each Saturday morning with a standing conflict.

My private tradition was to deliver Tyler and Joseph their breakfasts as they sat watching Saturday morning cartoons in the basement. Each week I made them a small plate of toasted waffles, sliced fruit, and some bacon or ham. I'd pour them each a cup of milk, then serve them as they sat on the floor laughing at Bugs Bunny, Elmer Fudd, and the Roadrunner.

"Why do you wait on them like that?!!" Michael would ask incredulously when I returned. "Let them get their own breakfast!!!"

Michael felt that the kids were living on Easy Street, with an overly indulgent mother.

"It's the only time I really pamper them, Michael - just let me enjoy it."

"Tyler is twelve - he's bigger than you now!"

"I know, but he's still a boy. He can be pampered once a week!"

"Annie, you're serving him milk in a SIPPY CUP!" Michael looked at me pointedly.

"I KNOW," I said with as much dignity as I

could muster. "I'm not babying him. It has a lid so it won't spill."

A mother's eye can differ from a dad's. But I suspect the differences in Michael's and my parenting approach also have to do with our respective family cultures. My three younger sisters and I were raised by upright parents who valued routine and order. Every Monday, our mother put out cold cereal for breakfast. Tuesdays followed with French toast, Wednesdays with fried eggs, etc. For lunch, even into our high school years, we each received a sack lunch with our name neatly penciled on the bag in Mom's loopy cursive. Mom and Dad provided for my sisters and me a loving and predictable environment, conscientiously shaped for our nurturing and growth.

Until I met Michael, I never pictured how different some families might be from mine.

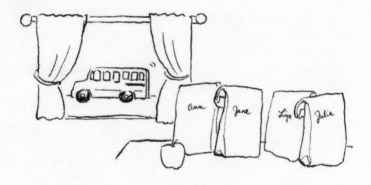

Mike

Bridget was a patient of mine who, like me, was born in July. She came to my office that month, and we started comparing notes. We agreed on the obvious advantage to a July birthday, that it's midway between Christmases.

Bridget told me that when she was a little girl, her mother used to say all the beautiful fireworks in the sky were to celebrate her birthday. Bridget was crushed when she finally realized it was a family myth. She asked me if my mother had told me something similar.

Her question made me laugh. The stories Chris and I heard from our mother were a different sort. For example, the summer we were five years old, Mom told us that the ice cream truck, with its tinkling song and bell, was the Boogey Man coming to get us.

We couldn't understand why the other neighborhood kids ran outside every time the Boogey Man rang his bell. But Chris and I weren't waiting to find out. We ran into the house and hid in the closet.

Our aunt came to visit one day and wondered aloud to my mother why Chris and I were so frightened. Mary explained in a fit of giggles. My aunt was appalled. Taking pity on us, she let us in on the secret and bought us each a cone.

I broached the Boogey Man story the other day to ascertain my mother's rationale. How could a mother lie to her helpless children? The memory made my mom giggle all over again.

"What can I say?" she said when she had finished laughing. "I was a smart mother. No annoying kids begging for money for the ice cream man!"

My mother doesn't like conflict. Mary was born in China during World War II, and her earliest memories are of bombing and death. She came to America when her father became a translator for the fledging United Nations in New York after the war. After this stormy childhood, what she craved most was peace and quiet.

Instead, she was blessed with twin sons and an Italian husband who agreed with the adage, *Boys will be boys*. Whenever Chris and I came to physical blows - not an uncommon event - my father would simply glance over and tell us to "take it outside." Black eyes, bloody noses, BB gun injuries, even a few incidents involving knives and arrows, are part of my brother's and my repertoire of "growing up" stories.

Perhaps conflict is inevitable when a future doctor grows up with a future attorney.

I suspect that, deep down, Mary had been hoping for a baby girl and was bummed out she'd had twin boys instead. My suspicions are based on a conversation I had with her when I was in medical school studying multiple gestation. "Were you happy when you found out you were having twin boys, Mom?" I asked her.

"No," Mary said matter-of-factly. "I was hoping for a baby girl, and I was bummed out I was getting twin boys instead."

Because I have cared for so many women and witnessed their struggles, I can't blame my mother for her Boogey Man strategy, or for expressing resentment about no baby girl. Growing a human being inside your body is physically demanding, and getting that human being out is even harder. But the most difficult task of all is everyday motherhood - nurturing that human being as he or she grows into independence. In comparison, fatherhood is a lightweight imitation.

I consider it a blessing that I get to take care of women.

But I am grateful to God I am a guy.

Is he GONE?

Family Fables

What do you mean, "The Tooth Fairy's on strike?"

Ann

Every December, I boot Michael and the boys out the door on a Saturday afternoon, their assigned mission to bring home our Christmas tree. This officially opens the season of Michael's and my traditional Yuletide Argument.

"Annie, I'm going to get a five-foot tree this time – it will be less work for you."

"Michael, I want an eight-foot tree – it looks better in the window."

"Annie, real trees are messy. I'm going to get you a beauooo-tiful artificial tree. Then you won't have to wait for us every year to buy a real one - you can just get it out of the attic and put it together yourself!"

"Michael, *please* – PLEASE *do not* get an artificial tree! Buying a Christmas tree is your ONLY CHRISTMAS JOB! Can't you do it for once without complaining!!?"

"I'm not complaining." He grinned. "I'm offering... suggestions."

It took me years to realize Michael was just

entertaining himself.

When my sisters and I were kids, Mom led the holiday celebrations by unearthing every decoration, store-bought or handmade, acquired since the time I was a baby. We decked the house with nativity scenes, Santas and greenery, and in the living room, an obscenely over-tinseled Christmas tree.

The climax of the season arrived on Christmas Eve when Dad sat before the ebbing fire and read aloud the Bible nativity story. This was the one holiday ritual my sisters and I clung to as adults, corralling the children and our lucky husbands into the living room each year to hear a Christmas Eve bedtime story read to them by their reluctant father-in-law.

The husbands tolerated this only slightly better than the kids.

I wanted Tyler and Joseph to experience every bit of the magic from my Christmas Past. Perhaps due to my elaborate efforts, Tyler persisted in believing in Santa Claus past the usual age. It wasn't until he entered fifth grade that he finally began to have some doubts about the Man in the Red Suit.

That autumn, my mother and I were home schooling Tyler, to give him a break from public school (or maybe to give public school a break from Tyler). Mom and I conspired that one of his semester "finals" would be memorizing and reciting the poem "'Twas the Night Before Christmas."

From start to finish, it took a good five minutes, a task he was required to perform in front of the entire family on Christmas Eve, as part of his year end grade.

As the holiday season progressed, Tyler began asking me point blank if there really was a Santa Claus. He declared he wanted to know the truth. I began to feel dishonest feeding him the children's story. Finally, one day I admitted the truth.

"Tyler, you're right: there isn't an actual Santa. But Santa's spirit is very much alive! And every year he's with us when we celebrate the birth of Christ and give presents to all the people we care about (etc., etc...)"

Tyler was crushed. The revelation shook him to the core, and he seized the opportunity to question the existence of God. "What ELSE have you lied to me about?" he asked me accusingly, days later. "Is GOD a lie, too?" It was a mother's worst nightmare. I wrestled with the horrible conviction that I had irrevocably damaged the spiritual faith of my firstborn son.

Finally Tyler put forward the biggest item on his list of Santa Grievances. From the time he was a small boy, Tyler had maintained a firm policy of executing the minimum amount of work required for any given task. "And you know, Mom, that's the part that makes me the maddest! I had to memorize a WHOLE poem about Santa Claus - and it's all just a LIE!

"What a waste of time," he muttered.

Mike

It was hard to match Ann's enthusiasm for childhood traditions, although I admit I was an excited young father when my oldest son, Tyler, lost his first tooth. Tyler's eyes grew wide when I explained what would happen once he fell asleep. Eagerly I anticipated my part in this ritual. But when I snuck into his room that night, I couldn't find the tooth under his pillow, no matter how much I felt around. When I jammed my toe on his bed frame, I hopped out of his bedroom, fearful I'd awaken Tyler with my un-Fairylike expletives.

The next morning, as soon as it was light, I snuck back in and successfully replaced the tooth with a dollar. Tyler was disappointed when he looked under his pillow. It seems that the Tooth Fairy had bestowed a more generous *five* dollars on his friend. I explained to Tyler that he received less money because he didn't place his tooth in a plastic bag, which helps the Tooth Fairy find it.

From then on, the Tooth Fairy's nighttime job was a breeze, and Tyler invariably found the preferred denomination of currency under his pillow.

I saved all my children's teeth in a box in my study. Partly it was sentiment that kept me from throwing the teeth away. It was also because they cost me so much money.

Joseph stumbled upon my collection of teeth when he was nine. He confronted me with an air of making light conversation: "Dad, I was looking through your office, and I notice you have a *close personal relationship* with the Tooth Fairy."

I laughed. "When did you stop believing in the Tooth Fairy, anyway?" I asked.

There was a long pause while Joseph pondered my question. "Well – just now, Dad," he answered.

Oops.

The next time Joseph lost a tooth, he proudly showed it to me. There was a large blood clot on it. He had pulled the loose tooth out of his mouth early because he needed the extra money.

"That's great, Joseph," I answered. "Put it in a plastic bag under your pillow, and we'll see what the Tooth Fairy will do tonight."

Joseph was all business. "I want my five bucks *now*," he said.

I glanced at the germ-infested tooth Joseph held in the palm of his hand. Joseph wore a particularly unappealing look on his face that seemed to say, "Pay up now, Mr. Tooth Fairy, you Big Faker!"

I didn't feel much love for my preadolescent son. At the moment, he reminded me of the spoiled girl Veruca from *Willy Wonka and the Chocolate Factory*, singing "I want it NOW!"

Echoing in my mind was the refrain sung by the prophetic orange-faced Oompa Loompas:

Who do you blame when your kid is a BRAT
Pampered and spoiled like a Siamese Cat?
Blaming the kids is a lion of shame
You know exactly WHO'S to BLAME:
The Mother and the Father!

I resisted the urge for a direct confrontation and opted instead for levity. "Joseph, I don't know if you follow the financial markets, but rising oil prices have bottomed out the used tooth market," I explained seriously. "That tooth of yours is only worth a nickel."

Joseph grew angry. "Dad, give me my money!"

"Sorry, Joseph," I said with a smile. "The commodities market can be brutal."

Joseph stormed off in a huff. The notably unattractive behavior only firmed my resolve. Thus began the Strike of the Tooth Fairy. Joseph could keep his used tooth for all I cared; I had plenty and yet to find a single buyer.

But the passage of a few days seemed to give Joseph a change of heart. A more charming child reappeared in my life. Joseph gave me a big hug before I tucked him into bed. He quietly showed me his tooth in a plastic bag. As I watched, he placed it under his pillow and expressed his hope that the Tooth Fairy was back on the job.

Later, I snuck into Joseph's room when he was asleep. The snot-nosed lines on his preadolescent face had relaxed into a visage of wondrous beauty. I thought about the ten-year-old ultrasound photo of Joseph I kept on my desk, an image from when he was only an inch long. I prayed at Joseph's bedside with gratitude for the privilege of being a father, and asked for guidance not to screw him up too much.

I also did the Tooth Fairy thing.

Ultimately, it was a financial decision. I figured since Joseph was a priceless gift from God, a dirty tooth yanked from his head had to be worth five bucks.

Joking Around

Sorry, honey. I meant that water balloon for the kids.

Ann

I knew Michael loved our boys, but sometimes, just like his parents, he didn't mind shaking up the kids with a good trick. This sometimes upset me. I worried Tyler and Joseph would be scarred.

One summer evening when Tyler was seven, Michael took the family out for ice cream. He bought each of us a cone, and then asked Tyler for a taste.

Tyler looked worried. He was familiar enough with his father to be cautious about sharing his scoop of Mint Chocolate Chip. Michael promised to take only "a little taste." Anxiously, Tyler held out his cone. Michael pursed his lips for a tiny sample. Then, like a creature from a horror movie, he enlarged his mouth in mesmerizing slow motion until it engulfed the entire scoop of ice cream, sucking the remnants from the depths of the cone.

Michael closed his mouth. He pulled the cone away from his face. It was empty. He handed it back to Tyler.

Tyler's jaw dropped. "DADDY!" he squawked. I

was horrified. Tyler began a mixture of laughing and crying. I looked over at Michael. His cheeks bulging, he appeared enormously amused, and I watched as he swallowed Tyler's ice cream, smiling all the while like a Cheshire cat.

My husband was a bully.

Tyler was still laughing a little, but continued to look forlornly at his empty cone. A few minutes passed before Michael tired of the joke, and then he bought Tyler another. This time it was a double.

It was years before I saw that perhaps this kind of play wasn't mean-spirited – and that eventually it might serve to give the boys a certain resilience.

When Tyler was ten, we went out for a family movie night. It had grown dark by the time we piled into the van to drive home. After we pulled out, Michael and I in the front and Joseph in the back, we were halfway home when we heard Joseph pipe up, "Where's Tyler?"

Michael and I both laughed, and I looked over my shoulder at Joseph to acknowledge the joke – when I saw that in fact Tyler's seat *was* empty. He hadn't gotten into the car with the rest of us. We'd left our child alone in the parking lot at night.

Michael broke the speed limit driving back. Within a mile we came upon Tyler jogging along the road home, a half-smile on his face.

We apologized shakily, but Tyler was unfazed.

"Well... I thought it was a little weird," he said, as he buckled himself in. "But I was also thinking, 'That was a pretty good joke, Daddy.'"

Mike

The year the boys were seven and ten, I asked for Ann's help playing an April Fools' joke on them. I told her what I had in mind, and although she wasn't crazy about it, she agreed to play along.

Sunrise on the big day found me crawling like a Ninja across the floor of Tyler's bedroom. With barely a sound, I rolled on to my back and shifted my body directly beneath his bed. I took a deep breath, and then, using all my strength, began shaking the entire bed frame in rapid tremors.

Annie's timing was perfect. At the same

moment, she burst into the bedroom. "Tyler!" she shouted. "Get up! It's an earthquake! It's an earthquake! Go downstairs – HURRY!!'

Tyler hardly moved. "It's okay, Mom," he mumbled, still half asleep. "It's just Dad under my bed."

I was demoralized. I had bruised my knees and scraped my back getting under the bed. But it was not going to be for nothing. Nursing my wounded pride, I hushed Ann and went to the next room. "Let's try it on Joseph."

But by the time I had crawled under Joseph's bed, Ann reported from the doorway that Joseph was smiling, his eyes closed, pretending to sleep.

Luckily, I had prepared a backup trick the night before. Placing a rubber band around the kitchen sink nozzle so it would spray as soon as the water was turned on, I had carefully swiveled it in the precise direction to douse the face of whoever of my beloved offspring washed his hands first.

Tyler came downstairs still half asleep, his first stop the bathroom.

"Would you please flush the toilet," I reminded him from the kitchen, "and wash your hands." It was hard to hide the eagerness in my voice. I watched Tyler as he came over to stand by his preferred sink in the kitchen and reach for the soap. He stopped, looked at the faucet, and yawned.

"You know, Dad," he said with a trace of patronization, "if you use scotch tape, it won't show as much."

I wasn't in the mood for advice. "Just be quiet, and let's wait for Joseph," I replied testily.

Tyler, in typical ten-year-old fashion, continued to explain why scotch tape would have been smarter. Annoyed, I began to argue.

"AAUGHH!" screeched Ann. Oops. While I was distracted, Annie had turned on the water and her pajamas were now soaked.

She was not amused. I apologized profusely, but Ann didn't believe she was not the intended victim.

Well, at least I'd gotten someone.

But my real quarry was Tyler. He was just too cocky for his own good. I spent the day mulling it over, playing a few jokes to pass the day. Pregnant patients made the easiest targets.

*Gosh, I hope you have **two** girls' names picked out.*

Or, *Wow, we haven't had triplets in the practice in four or five years.*

Back at home that evening, Tyler wouldn't fall for anything. I found myself growing amateurish in my desperation.

"There's a spider on your shoulder!"

"Your teacher just called. You're in trouble!"

Tyler just rolled his eyes disdainfully. April Fools' was obviously beneath him. Indeed, he hadn't played a single joke on me. I finally gave up, and I trudged upstairs to go to bed. Just as Ann and I climbed between the sheets, we were met by an impediment.

Tyler had short-sheeted our bed.

Ann was dead tired. She began to complain and laugh simultaneously as she proceeded to strip the bedcovers to remake the bed. I tried to shush her so Tyler wouldn't have the satisfaction of knowing his trick had succeeded.

But it was too late. I could hear him snickering outside our bedroom door.

My mind was unsettled. Although I was tired, I lay awake in bed for a while, unable to sleep. Finally, after some honest introspection, I came to one resolution which allowed me to drift off at last.

Just wait 'til next year.

Seriously, Now

C'mon, sweetie, that was funny. When are you going to start speaking to me again, anyway?

Ann

I was a nervous young mother when Tyler was born, with no experience and no family nearby. To me, this vulnerable being appeared to be in constant danger. In his crib, he could stop breathing. At the grocery store, he might catch a fatal bug.

And in the bathtub? He might get stuck in the drain and drown.

For Tyler's first bath, my hands were shaking as I held open the baby book, tensely following the directions step by step - including testing the water temperature with my elbow, just as the author recommended. I was worried I would scald this tiny person. I was worried I would drop him. I was worried I would let Tyler's face slip under the water where he would somehow asphyxiate instantly.

Michael was nearing the end of his first year of OB-GYN residency. After ten months, he had pulled hundreds of babies from their mothers' bodies and was confident in the basic durability of newborns. He noticed my anxiety around Tyler and agreed to help me bathe him.

He ran to get the video camera.

Michael pointed the lens and zoomed in on my shaking hands. He began to lecture in a vaguely British accent, narrating like a nature show host. "The young mother is nervous as she tests the bath water with her elbow. She finds it acceptable...she picks up the baby...careful, careful...CAREFUL! That was a close one - she almost dropped him there..."

I glared at Michael, but that only egged him on. He continued, "The joy of the young mother bathing her child is evident. Observe how she holds the small head out of the water while trying to soap the tiny baby's limbs. This delicate balancing act would be easier – if only she had someone to help her..."

I couldn't shove him out of the room without setting Tyler down -

But at least I wasn't nervous anymore.

I was infuriated.

We sometimes watch the video at Christmas when we have the camera out. Michael still finds it funny, and I still become annoyed. But without a doubt, it documents my congenital tendency to take some things a bit more seriously than Michael.

I suppose it still comes down to family culture. A few Christmases ago, my parents and Michael's came over for dinner. They spent some time talking in the entryway while Michael and I were preparing the food. When my father-in-law finally came into the dining room, we saw that his hair was tinted a strange pink shade. It had also been molded into a distinct peak at the top of his head.

"WHAT is the matter with your hair?!!" Michael started laughing.

Phil played it straight. "*What?* You don't like it?"

Mary started giggling hysterically. "Phil thought he should be festive for Christmas dinner. He asked for the red food coloring, and then he wanted help so he could dye his hair red."

We all agreed it was an outstanding look. Until that moment, my reticent parents, polite to the last, hadn't said a word. Now that the cat was out of the bag, my mother smiled in relief.

"Well, I noticed *something,* but I didn't want to say anything and make Phil self-conscious." She paused and said seriously. "You know, I just thought it was just one of those bad dye jobs."

Mike

My mother owns a long-haired, ill-tempered cat that gives me asthma attacks. This animal is named "Bastet" after the Egyptian cat goddess, but I dispense with pleasantries and call her "Asbestos" instead, after the carcinogenic insulation material.

Once when my parents had returned from a vacation, Joseph and I offered to pick up Asbestos at the vet's as a favor for my mom. Joseph was twelve and old enough to stay home by himself, but I often grabbed him or Tyler on my weekend errands so we could have some time together.

As we entered the vet's office, I was pleasantly surprised to spy two cookie jars on the counter. I have a weak spot for cookies. Obviously, this was my reward for a good deed.

Joseph headed into the back with the receptionist to look at some puppies, and I was alone for a few minutes. With happy anticipation, I lifted the lid off the first jar and looked inside. Dog biscuits! My heart sank. With diminished hopes, I lifted the lid from the second jar. To my surprise, it was filled with miniature chocolate chip cookies! Now *that* made sense: cookies for the dog, cookies for the owner – everybody's happy.

Still alone, I palmed a modest handful. I didn't

want anybody to think I was a pig. I popped them in my mouth and began happily crunching. My taste buds staged an immediate protest. These were the most disgusting chocolate chip cookies I'd ever tasted. Suddenly it came to me: they were not cookies - they were dog biscuits in disguise!

As my mouth filled with crumbling dog treats, Joseph and the receptionist reappeared. *This* was a problem. How was I going to spit out the biscuits without everybody knowing? I had no trouble picturing the veterinary staff laughing it up for days after I left. *Can you believe that dumb guy? A whole mouthful of doggie cookies!* And Joseph would be mocking me all the way home.

I held my mouth shut, endeavoring to stanch the awful taste, and wondered what to do. I started padding my pockets as though looking for my cell phone. *Oh my gosh, I must have left it in the car.* I grabbed my keys and headed for the exit. My plan was to open my car door, sit in the seat, and spit the dog biscuits out into the parking lot where no one could see.

But Dr. Calder walked out of the back, carrying my mother's stupid cat. He motioned me over. Inwardly, I groaned. My mouth still full, I sauntered over with elaborate nonchalance and feigned a smile. Dr. Calder opened Bastet's medical chart to show me her low potassium level. He began explaining what causes this condition and what should be done.

Who cares about the cat's potassium level?!! I wanted to shout. *Just throw Asbestos in my car so I can spit out those poison cookies! Besides, everyone knows a banana a day will fix the cat's potassium just fine!!*

Instead, I nodded sagely and pretended to listen. I was concentrating on swallowing the doggie treats without gagging. One last swallow, and it was over.

But as Joseph and I were leaving, inspiration struck. I'd get Joseph to eat a few of those cookies, too. It was the perfect family bonding opportunity.

Casually, I gestured to the second cookie jar and mentioned to Joseph he should grab a handful "for the road." I waited halfway out the door, holding the cat carrier with an expression on my face that conveyed the usual parental impatience that he was taking too long. Hiding my eagerness, I watched Joseph lift the lid and peer into the jar. I couldn't wait for him to pop a handful of those disgusting things into his mouth.

Joseph stared at the camouflaged chocolate chip cookies for a long moment. And then he looked at me and rolled his eyes.

"Dad, those are dog biscuits!" he said, shaking his head. "How dumb do you think I am?"

2

Communication

Ann

*When something's wrong,
it's important for us to keep
communication lines open
so we can work it out.
Now, let's listen to what
each of us has to say.
Michael, you first.*

Mike

I just want everyone
to shut up.

Apologizing
**Just say you're sorry ten more times,
and we'll call it even.**

Ann

Four months before the day of our wedding, Michael and I had a serious quarrel. He was having doubts about getting married. Maybe we were too young. Maybe we were rushing things.

Maybe we shouldn't go through with the wedding.

The ceremony was sixteen weeks away. I had told everyone the date. I had a diamond ring on my finger! But in the midst of our escalating argument, I suddenly saw with total clarity that under no circumstances should I marry this... *jerk*.

I broke the engagement.

And Michael had the gall to look relieved.

I was heartbroken. All my bright dreams, gone. But that night as I lay soaking my pillow with tears, I began to realize that this was not the end. God had a plan for me, and I would march on with my life alone. I felt a great sense of Peace, lifting me out of my sorrow, and I knew that this was the right decision.

The next morning I woke up to the sound of Michael knocking on my door. He'd had a change of heart. He asked me to reconsider. He begged me to take him back. I had changed his life, I had introduced him to God, I was beautiful, he was undeserving. I wasn't sure. He continued to apologize. I still wasn't sure.

Finally he hit the right combination from the list of his transgressions, and I accepted his apology.

It only took him nine hours.

Do you, Michael, solemnly promise to apologize frequently and often to your wife?

Mike

The anatomical differences between a husband and a wife are nothing compared to the differences in what a man and woman find interesting to talk about.

Ann is an artsy type. For years she has been in a book club with a dozen other women. They meet monthly at a restaurant for dinner and high-brow conversation where together they dissect the themes from the month's book selection in what I imagine is enthusiastic non-stop conversation.

"I was fascinated how the author demonstrated so poignantly the love between...blah, blah, blah..."

"Me too...and I was filled with wonder about...blah, blah, blah..."

"And don't forget in chapter seven when...blah, blah, blah..."

Many intelligent words are spoken and insightful phrases turned in conversation that I'm sure on some spiritual level advances the collective wisdom of humankind.

But for me, it all boils down to a lot of *blah, blah, blah...*

Just imagining all the gabbing that goes on in that restaurant gives me a migraine. This is a group of book-reading, wine-drinking, intelligent women who meet monthly just to talk to each other.

I feel sorry for the waiters.

For some reason, Ann has never invited me to join her book club. But when this oversight is finally corrected, I know exactly how I will decline: "Look, Ann – the last time I was forced into boring conversation about a boring book, it wasn't called 'Book Club' – it was called 'High School English.' "

Sadly, I know everything that is said at book club. When Ann comes home excited by the evening's gabfest, she tells me all about it. Her eyes shine bright blue as she recounts blow-by-blow who said what and how brilliant it was and why. As a husband, I admit it's a pleasant experience to be around a happy wife. Lord knows it beats the alternative.

I like watching Ann's face glow with enthusiasm. I like listening to her laugh. But sometimes, when she recounts all the intelligent things said at book club and shares with me all the hilarity, I find myself at wit's end determining the most polite way to get her to shut up.

It's not that I am an intellectual caveman. It's because I am trying to fall asleep. Picture a wide-awake wife sitting up in bed, words pouring out of her mouth faster than thought, next to an exhausted husband with his head on the pillow, endeavoring to time his grunts so his wife doesn't think he is ignoring her. I have learned the hard way that it's rude to snore when your wife is talking to you. It's also not acceptable to groan in despair when your wife is midsentence and to cover your head protectively with a pillow.

I don't remember doing those things, but after a

blissful night's sleep I have sometimes awakened to a full recounting of my transgressions in the morning. The expression on my wife's face over morning coffee has not been the enthusiastic or happy one glimpsed the evening before.

Of the various outcomes, I've found I prefer the "I am really angry with you" outburst over the "you hurt my feelings" variation any day.

Anger is easier for a man to handle and goes far better with the cup of morning Joe.

My strategies have evolved over the course of our marriage. My first line of defense is the Rhetorical Question: *Why in the world do you talk to me when I am falling asleep, anyway?*

Next in line, the Earnest Explanation: *I was in surgery all day...*

Sometimes the Offhand Joke can be applied: *Can't I just go with you to book club next time so I don't miss anything?*

At this point, I've had plenty of practice apologizing for all kinds of shortcomings over the years. When the "you hurt my feelings" comes to the fore, the morning conversation tends to go poorly. I don't want to hurt my wife's feelings - although sometimes I can get a tad bit resentful.

I just slept great, and I'm ready to tackle the day! I'll take my coffee black - hold the sugar, hold the cream, and most of all - hold the Guilt Trip.

When it comes to apologizing, I still don't always get the tone right on my first go. After twenty-five years of practice, Ann can hear my eyeballs rolling in their sockets. Occasionally, if I'm especially clumsy or irritable, I'll hurt her feelings more and more - until finally, I have no alternative except the last resort -

The full sensation and subsequent expression of Genuine Remorse.

Only then does my apology echo the sincerity a man feels toward the woman he has loved through the years:

"The wonder of your beauty brings Love and God into my life, and only in my incompleteness do I hurt you."

Making Time to Talk
Can't we just watch TV instead?

Ann

Michael and I had a long distance relationship for our entire three-year courtship leading up to our wedding. During that time we communicated constantly; we poured our love into hundreds of letters and thousands of minutes on the phone. Michael became my best friend, and we began and ended each day talking to each other.

When married life finally brought us together, the torrent of communication subsided to a more sustainable flow. Within two years, Michael entered medical school. The hours of study required were brutal; he buried himself in his books.

And our communications dwindled to a trickle.

Not long into Michael's first semester, my art business slowed, and we were facing our first financial crisis. Michael was cramming for a major round of exams, but the problem was urgent, and I wanted his feedback. "Michael, I wonder if we can talk about a money issue..."

He groaned. "Sweetie, this is the *worst* possible

time, RIGHT before exams."

A few weeks later, I made another attempt to communicate about our money troubles. This one was also met with a groan: "Sheesh, right after exams! Can't I just enjoy this time a little bit?"

Finally I timed the discussion for what I thought was a mundane week in Michael's academic schedule. Which met with: "Hey! NOT right in the middle of my studying! I've got a LOT of work to do!!"

I exploded. "Okay, smarty pants – not BEFORE exams, not DURING exams, and not IN BETWEEN! WHEN exactly is it we're supposed to talk?"

Michael thought a moment and then smiled a little. "Okay, I'm sorry. I guess I'm just trying to not have this conversation at all."

I wish I could say that after this experience, I discovered the magic formula for timing difficult conversations. However, that would not be true. The one thing I did acquire was a certain sensitivity to timing.

Nowadays, it's the morning hours when Michael mentally prepares for surgery that are off limits for emotionally challenging discussions. And as the demands of my life have increased, Michael has returned the favor - by becoming skilled in the reading of the Wife-Stress Barometer.

Mike

Almost every day I see at least one patient pushed to the breaking point by life stresses. Conflicting yet urgent demands of children, marriage, work, and older parents dog them every day. Sometimes women need to hear it's okay to take a break.

Ann is no exception.

It was a typical Saturday morning, and already Ann had been working for several hours at the computer, sitting ramrod straight in her chair. No doubt she was stressed out, with too many projects on her plate. It seemed like the perfect time for a surprise I had been planning.

With a flourish, I invited Ann to come with me to my office. She raised her eyebrows. "Can't it wait?"

When I said no, I was met with a frown. Reluctantly, Ann accompanied me upstairs. Once in my office, I moved to my computer and selected a song I had recently added to my play list. The music began, and everything was ready. I asked Ann to dance.

Lionel Richie and Diana Ross's duet "Endless Love" was all the rage back in the day. I remember dancing to the song, feeling deeply in love. The piano played softly, and then the lyrics came...

"My love... there's only you in my life... the only thing that's bright..." What a charming romantic I was!

Ann rolled her eyes and reminded me she had been busy. Her reaction surprised me. I thought she would gaze adoringly into my eyes with the look I remembered from years before. But Ann's body remained stiff. Instead of feeling like the high school quarterback dancing with the head cheerleader, I began to feel like the nerd the girls may feel sorry for but avoid anyway.

I became annoyed. *Fall in love with me again, why don't you already?* Tactfully, I expressed concern that our once special memories of dancing to our song meant nothing to her now.

"Our song?" Ann pulled her head back to look me in the face. "We never danced to that song - I never even LIKED that song!"

Oops.

This was an awkward revelation.

Well, at least that explained why she wasn't melting in my arms. I could feel Ann's body tensing even more as the implication of my mistaken memory became clear to us both. Our dance became more and more stilted, until we were essentially standing still in the middle of my office.

I could feel the question coming.

"So, Michael," Ann opened, "which one of your 'past loves' did you enjoy this wonderful song with?"

Funny you should ask, my dear, I thought to myself. *I was just wondering the same thing myself.*

A surgeon in the middle of an operation would call this "getting into unexpected bleeding." It had started as the perfect plan - play a song of tender memories, and instantly transform Ann from the "I have too many things to do" stressed-out woman to the "I am so lucky to have you as a husband" happy wife. A beautiful Saturday afternoon would follow, with Ann gazing at me adoringly even if I was just scratching myself.

Now all I wanted was to get this angry hellion out of my office without causing any more emotional damage. The music continued to play as I held my jealous wife in my arms. This was not "Endless Love." This was "Endless Dance." *Would you please shut up already, Lionel?*

"It wasn't that we ever danced to this song," I explained disingenuously. "It's just that whenever I hear it, I think about you and how much I love you." It was the right thing to say, a good line, really – but I delivered it half-heartedly, in a perfunctory, oh-let-me-just-say-it-and-get-it-over-with sort of way.

Ann suddenly relaxed and surprised me by laughing out loud. She seemed delighted by my obvious lack of candor.

"Oh, really?" She batted her eyelashes coquettishly. "Do you really mean it, or are you just trying to flatter me?"

"Oh, yes," I responded, smiling at her like a used

car salesman. "I wouldn't lie to you, my darling."

Ann laughed again. And remarkably, she rested her face against my chest with a smile on her face.

Her body relaxed. "I'm sorry I've been so stressed out lately," she said a few moments later.

My plan had worked after all! Ann had actually melted in my arms. What a remarkable mystery is womanhood.

In retrospect, I have to say I still don't completely understand, and I can only guess why Ann softened up. Perhaps she was simply being generous. In our years of marriage, I have always been grateful for unforeseen moments of God's grace – wherever I have found them.

I suppose it's not choosing the right song that matters most. Sometimes, you get credit just for the effort.

Kids: Walking and Talking

Two years teaching them to walk and talk.
The next sixteen getting them to sit down and shut up.

Ann

When Tyler was six years old, he became obsessed with Japanese trading cards that featured tiny cartoon monsters called "Pokemon." The characters had impossible names like "Raichu" and "Pikachu." Tyler was never without his stack of cards, and he left a trail of Pokemon everywhere he went – under the table, in the cracks of the furniture cushions.

The Pokemon onslaught dominated our family conversation.

Mom? Mom? Who is your favorite Pokemon? Dad, who would you rather fight with, Blastoise or Charizard? Why? Do you want to know who I'd rather fight?

I couldn't help but remember Tyler's infant days. He gurgled, bleated, and honked, and we were free to imagine that all the thoughts he was struggling to say were sweet and interesting. Then he started forming real words, like "NO!" and "I don't WANT dat!" And within a couple of years, whole paragraphs were pouring out, and thus ended our blissful parental wondering.

One day Michael couldn't take the Pokemon barrage any longer. When he got home from work, Tyler ran up as usual to get his father's attention.

"Dad, Dad, can I tell you something?"

To my surprise, Michael smiled serenely. "Tyler, you can tell me anything you want - so long as it has absolutely *nothing* to do with Pokemon."

His internal struggle was visible on Tyler's face as he marshaled his concentration. Finally he blurted, "Daddy - what's your favorite Pokemon?"

"TYLER!! I said tell me anything you want – as long as it's NOT about Pokemon!!'

Tyler gave him an exasperated look. "I'm NOT telling you," he said. "I'm *asking*."

Mike

The unhealthy things in life - like pigging out on popcorn at the movies - are sometimes the most fun. The trick is to offset unhealthy choices with healthy ones. So on a hot summer Saturday when the boys asked me to take them to the movies, I agreed...

On one condition: we walk.

Some might say that making your kids walk three miles to the movie theater under the hot Georgia sun is torture, plain and simple. Others might argue that listening to two kids whining for three miles is a torture even worse. In a grand cosmic sense, I suppose it was only fair: I exercised my children's bodies, they exercised my patience.

The main benefit of an hour's walk over a five minute drive was that we noticed things we wouldn't otherwise. Hills were the main thing. When it's a hundred degrees outside, your perceptions of terrain changes are mysteriously heightened.

Tyler and Joseph complained and complained, of course. But they also talked about other things - which teachers they liked, which classmates were bullies, which neighborhood hangouts were most fun, even the metaphysical *what-do-you-want-to-be-when-you-grow-up?*

As we neared the theater, we discovered the road

crossed a beautiful stream. I'd whizzed past it a thousand times, but had never noticed it before. From our steel and concrete vantage fifty feet above the surface, we paused to watch the water.

Tyler and Joseph began to spit.

Then a beaver swam by with a stick in his mouth. The boys stared in wonder.

The last hundred-yard stretch was straight uphill. I sprinted with the boys, endeavoring to appear unfazed by the exercise. But I got dizzy in the end and had to rest my hands on my knees to catch my breath. Hard-earned tickets in hand, the three of us entered the lobby at last, where we were enveloped by a manmade oasis of glorious air conditioning.

We sauntered to the concession stand. I tried to talk the kids out of "butter" on the popcorn. The butter I know comes from cows, and is not pumped from a stainless steel container by an adolescent clerk with blue spiked hair. But in the end, not only did I capitulate on the "butter," I ordered the overpriced "Jumbo Combo," complete with refillable drinks.

I told the boys, *To heck with dinner - Let's refill that bucket and drink as many times as we want!* They had big smiles on their faces as they carried their goodies to the theater. They said I was the coolest.

I can't take credit - I just wanted to get my money's worth.

The movie was okay, I guess – probably an action hero flick. I've long since forgotten.

But our walk together – that, I'll remember for a long time.

Middle School Blues

Worse than the Terrible Twos.

Ann

As the boys progressed in grade school, they each became more and more unhappy – especially Tyler. By the time he was ten, he was coming home every afternoon with a new "hate" list.

"How was school today, Tyler?" I would ask hopefully.

"I hate history class. It's just such a waste of time!!

"...and I hate Mrs. So-and-so. She just likes to torture us with homework for no reasons.

"...and I REALLY hate David. He just tries to beat me in math class. He thinks he's so great!"

Tyler's growing unhappiness kept me awake nights, and I drove Michael crazy wondering aloud where we had gone wrong and how we could have shaped Tyler's attitude into something more positive. Our once bright-eyed child wasn't "engaged" in his learning. He wasn't excited about the world.

I had enjoyed school myself. I couldn't relate to Tyler's anger. Every day I felt an unbearable inner tension as I tried to distract him from his dissatisfaction. I was desperate to find something he might be able to like. "Tyler... honey, isn't there ANYTHING you don't hate?"

He paused to consider the question seriously. "Well, recess. That's okay. I guess."

One afternoon when Tyler was raging against his life, I started crying. The tears welled up, despite my desire to maintain my equanimity.

Tyler's face changed expression. "Mom!! What's wrong?!"

"I'm sorry, Tyler - you're just so unhappy." I tried to wipe the tears away. "It's so hard for a mom to see her child in pain. That's all."

Tyler came over with a smile and awkwardly patted me on the back.

"Mom," he soothed. "Mom, don't take it so seriously." He looked me in the face, just as his dad does when I get upset. "Don't you know by now?" he asked. "I just like complaining!"

Mike

I was taking Tyler to school one morning and couldn't help but feel a surge of empathy for my son. Junior high school for me was awful. I wondered how he was holding up.

"How is it, Tyler," I opened in a low-key manner, "going to school with all those other twits?"

It didn't come out quite the way I meant it, but Tyler didn't miss a beat. "It's okay, Dad," he shot back. "And how is it in surgery, operating with all those other quacks?"

Quality time with your kids sure does change as they get older. Back in the years when they believed in Santa, the boys would race to the door to hug me when I came home. Those were good times. In the innocent eyes of your children, you can see the smile of God.

With a thirteen-year-old son, you need stronger glasses.

When we stopped at a red light along the way, Tyler asked me if I knew what a "bean dip" was. I did not. I should have noticed his smirk.

Tyler reached over and flicked the part of me I think of as rock hard chest muscle. It jiggled a little.

"Bean Dip!" Tyler shouted gleefully. He finished giggling and then kindly explained to me that he and his friends often did this to each other. "Boy, your chest moved more than Wesley's, and he's the weakest kid in school!"

Somehow I failed to see the humor. I communicated to Tyler that if he showed me a "bean dip" again, he would experience significant physical discomfort.

I remember thirteen being a tough age. I had a hard time myself. I didn't like myself very much and in later years have often wondered why. Was it insecurity, peer pressure, adolescent hormones...? But once I was living with a thirteen-year-old, I finally had the answer.

Thirteen-year-old boys are not that likeable.

I remembered being always eager to see my kids when I got home from work. But on that particular day, after driving Tyler to school, I had the melancholy realization that the golden years of fatherhood had come to an end. Forget about looking forward to seeing my thirteen-year-old son.

I just wanted a place to hide.

I had the perfect spot in our house. It was an upstairs office, about the size of a large closet. In it I had stashed boxes of past treasured possessions including comic books, a collection of assorted swords and knives, and even an eight-foot long African spear with matching shield.

Coincidentally, these were the exact items Ann had repeatedly encouraged me to throw away.

I spent a lot of time in my "hiding place" over the next couple of days, pulling out my old collections and lining my shelves and walls with comics and swords and knives. Barricaded in my room and surrounded by my treasures, I figured I was safe from attacks by my offspring.

It was like trying to repel bears with honey pots.

"This is pretty cool, Dad," Tyler wandered by one night, stopping to peruse the walls. "Can I come in and read your comics?"

And that's how my "hiding place" from my boys became a clubhouse instead. As time passed, the collectibles gave us plenty of food for conversation, with Tyler and Joseph showing interest in various things as they matured.

There were still a few rules: rudeness or misbehavior would lead to expulsion from the club -

And the first rule was carved in stone.

No bean dips allowed.

The Sound of Silence
Thirty seconds of actual conversation. A new record.

Ann

When the boys became teenagers, they headed straight for their video games as soon as they came home from school. I was lucky to get a hello.

Ironically, I missed the days of the boys' ceaseless chatter. At this point, I would have been grateful for even a few complaints. I started hanging around the kitchen mid-afternoons when the boys were due home from school, acting breezily unconcerned while doing something I had never done much before - bake homemade cookies. I wanted them to linger, even if it was only to lick a spoon of raw batter.

A typical afternoon might begin with Joseph, fresh off the bus, coming in through the door.

"Hey Joseph, how was your day?" I'd watch him silently dump his backpack on the table. I hoped he'd find the warm cookies tempting.

"Oh - hey, Mom. Good."

"Cool! Anything happen today worth mentioning?"

"Nope." He grabbed a handful of cookies, and peered into the fridge.

"What did you think about the new student lounge?"

"Not sure."

"I heard it was nice," I fished hopefully.

"Yeah, I heard that, too." Joseph opened the door to the basement. "Love ya. See ya, Mom!" I watched him disappear downstairs.

Elapsed conversation time: thirty seconds.

Mike

When I headed to the hospital on weekday mornings, I often left the house with one of the boys to drop off at school. One morning Joseph and I were about to leave in the car when, without explanation, he opened the passenger door and disappeared into the house. I hated being late for surgery and waited with growing impatience. *One more minute and you can walk...*

I drove Joseph to school whenever I could. I figured a teen can always use the extra sleep. More importantly, I knew he wasn't going to live in my house forever, and these moments together were precious and fleeting. Theoretically, our drives together were "quality family time."

But sometimes they felt less like "quality," and more like "stomach ulcer."

On that morning I backed out of the driveway into the street as a warning signal. Joseph emerged from the house. When he spotted my car's progress, he stopped and crossed his arms in disapproval. Reluctantly, he walked toward my car, adopting such a sluggish pace I couldn't help jerking the car forward another twenty feet. Joseph halted and glared. I gestured violently. He resumed walking even more slowly.

Angrily, I accelerated forward fifty yards to the end of the block. Joseph threw out both arms in a *"what's your problem?"* gesture, and dragged toward me like an angry snail.

I leaped out of the car and threw his book bag on the pavement. "You can walk to school, Joseph!" I shouted.

Two neighbors on a morning stroll smiled politely with raised eyebrows, eyeing me in my surgical scrubs, standing in the middle of the street yelling at my son fifty yards away.

Ann sometimes complained that I acted the same age as Joseph. But she was wrong. I acted at least three years older - plus I had a driver's license, so there.

The pace of daily life is a pressure cooker, sometimes causing us to boil over. I wanted to be on time for surgery; I wanted to give my son a ride. As long as he didn't keep me waiting, everything worked great.

But teenagers have their own agendas.

Joseph caught an extra half hour of sleep the mornings I drove him to school. In my mind's eye, I pictured him using the extra time for character-building activities - a few push-ups, some prayer time, maybe cleaning the garage... But in reality, when he finally made his way downstairs, he'd plop down on the couch, bury his face in the cushions, and moan about how tired he was.

His lackadaisical teen attitude felt like a personal affront. I'd watch in disbelief as Ann made this lazy moocher a hot breakfast. Eventually he'd mosey to the table to leisurely munch his morning repast.

It was enough to make you sick.

So on the way to school, I did the father-teenage son thing. I lectured Joseph. I chastised him. I endeavored to enlighten him about responsibility and effort.

Looking back, if I had been Joseph, I would have preferred the bus.

But Joseph expressed profound sadness whenever we didn't drive together. He lamented he didn't get to "spend enough time" with me. I suspect the truth was that he regretted losing his personal chauffeur. The only thing I was missing was the hat.

On this occasion, Joseph broke into a respectful jog once he saw his book bag on the street. I decided to give him a second chance. On the way to school I treated him to a long lecture on the importance of punctuality. I ended by insisting he apologize for keeping me waiting.

"Sir, I am sorry for making you late, Sir," he recited woodenly. The tone of his voice conveyed exactly what he meant - expletives and all.

I couldn't help but laugh.

I don't know what's more difficult: being a parent trying to raise a child, or being a child and putting up with a parent. It's probably an even toss-up. The real task is doing your best in the moment and enjoying the blessings of family in whatever way you can.

By the time I dropped Joseph off, we were laughing about something. He jumped out of the car with his bag and closed the car door. He reached through the window to give me a fist bump. I checked the clock and saw I was almost on schedule.

It had been quality family time after all.

Family Time

The only difficult part is spending it with family.

Ann

When Michael and his classmates entered medical school, one of their professors gave them an introductory lecture about the pressures of being a doctor and how to have a good family life.

This medical professor recommended a "family project." For his wife and three kids it was a sailboat, which the family crewed together.

Michael and I were captivated by the idea and enthusiastically agreed that a family project was a great idea. I'm not sure what Michael pictured. My childhood memories flashed with pictures of my sisters and me joining in family sing-alongs, taking nature hikes, and participating in a cornucopia of family Christmas traditions, like constructing gingerbread houses and making homemade gifts.

The Christmas after Michael and I were married, we went home to visit my family. There I got my first inkling that family activities might look different if Michael and I happened to have boys. My sisters and I were absorbed in making the annual Wallace gingerbread house. We began applying the usual gum drop shingles, one by one.

Michael, who was watching, started getting bored. He rummaged around in the refrigerator and, grabbing an extra large egg, cracked it into the sink.

Bringing over the jagged half shell, he pushed it straight into the smooth frosting "yard" surrounding the gingerbread house.

"There!" he said, obviously pleased with himself.

"What is it?" we asked. We were horrified. The whole thing was ruined.

He looked at us in disbelief. "Isn't that better?!" Seeing the dismay on our faces, he looked at us like we were idiots.

"It's a JACUZZI."

Years later, after Tyler and then Joseph came along, I eventually came to understand that the key question for the family activity was no longer, "How did it turn out?"

The question was, "Hey, did we have a good time?"

Mike

As a child, Ann spent many summer days with her sisters rambling through Midwest farm country, picking blackberries for their traditional family fruit cobbler. The recipe had been handed down through five generations from Great, Great Grandmother Cordelia Hutson.

Two decades later, when Ann and I moved to the then rural suburbs of Atlanta, Ann resolved to resurrect the family tradition. She located a large blackberry patch behind my neighbor David's house.
84

Every week in midsummer, she would disappear for a couple of hours, reappearing at home with a bucket of fresh blackberries. A couple hours later - voila! Grandma Cordelia's homemade blackberry cobbler.

Ann did all the work, the boys and I did most of the eating. It was a great summer tradition.

But a few years ago, my neighbor David had the blackberry bushes cut down. They blocked the view from his patio, he said, and he wanted a better vista. Ann related the tragedy that evening: "David tried to tell me those weren't blackberries. He said, *'Those are just ol' sticker bushes.'* " Ann rolled her eyes in mild disgust.

Frankly, I was surprised. I had no idea those ugly sticker bushes in David's yard grew blackberries. But the look on Ann's face told me to keep my mouth shut.

"Yes, dear," I nodded, "that David sure is an inconsiderate ignoramus!"

Fearful this was the swan song for our summer cobbler, I chimed in with a helpful suggestion. The plump blackberries at the local grocery were even better candidates than the ones Ann had been picking. I offered that a cobbler made with those berries might taste even *better* than the wild ones.

Ann didn't warm to my proposal. Picking berries was part of the "whole experience," she informed me curtly.

Fortunately, Grandma Cordelia's cobbler is a versatile dish, and any fruit will do. Persevering, Ann purchased blueberry bushes to plant in our front yard. Two short years later, the first harvest was ready. *Ta-*

da!! Grandma's fresh *blueberry* cobbler! Just like before, Ann did all the work, and the boys and I did most of the eating.

A great summer tradition lives on.

A few summers had passed when Joseph found blackberry bushes growing wild a mile from our house. Ann announced that blackberry picking would be a great *family* activity.

A mile of walking under the hot Georgia sun to pick blackberries off sticker bushes didn't sound like a fun family activity to me.

I tried to make Ann understand a critical distinction: I am a berry eater, not a berry picker.

It had been years since we had had blackberry cobbler, Ann responded, and a change from the blueberry might be fun.

I informed her that the blueberries she picked right in my front yard by herself were now my favorite. Furthermore, since I had thus far not picked any cobbler berries at all, my getting involved was breaking our longstanding summer tradition... And one shouldn't be rash when it comes to breaking tradition.

Ann wasn't buying it.

I got off the couch and roused the boys. It was a pretty long walk under the hot sun to the blackberry patch, and between the boys complaining, and Ann telling me what a great family experience we were having, I was pretty miserable. I felt a surge of anger toward my good friend and neighbor David: *Why oh why did you cut down those beautiful blackberry bushes in your backyard, you inconsiderate ignoramus?*

When we finally arrived at the sunny blackberry

patch, dotted with flitting birds and butterflies, we found many bushes, and they were indeed covered with blackberries. It was tricky reaching over the thorny branches to get the juiciest ones. I was glad Ann had made me wear long pants. The boys and I got into a healthy male competition about who could pick the most. And we laughed with immature satisfaction to hear the other fellow yelp when a sticker found its way to vulnerable skin.

In retrospect, it really *was* a good family activity.

And Ann was right – that evening, the blackberry cobbler topped with a scoop of vanilla ice cream was the best dessert I ever had.

It seems that Grandma Cordelia's recipe neglects to mention the most important ingredients – effort and love. For all we do in life, when we put these into the mix, it makes everything better.

3

Learning Tolerance

Ann

*Each of us looks at the world
through our own eyes.
We need to understand
each other's point of view
to live together
in a loving and tolerant way.*

Mike

Okay. Right now,
my point of view is
you're annoying me.

The Marriage Thermostat
From hot temper to cold shoulder.

Ann

I torture Michael and the boys with environmental lectures. I consider it a civic duty: Turn off the lights when you leave the room, don't leave the water running, use scrap paper, not new. Every morning after they leave, I circle through the house, sighing and turning off all the lights they've left on.

Our generation grew up during the energy crisis of the 70's. As oil and gas prices soared, Dad decided to inspire good conservation habits in my sisters and me with an activity he called "The Energy Game." For several months one winter, he doled out ten dimes to each of us on Sunday nights. Throughout the week, if any of us caught another leaving a room without turning off the light, we could extract from them a fine of one dime.

The more energy conscious we became, the bigger the payout.

My younger sisters Liza and Julie and I schemed and spied to confiscate each other's money. Jane, however, refused. Scowling, she flipped on extra lights and left them burning, unloading her dimes as quickly as possible so she could forget about the whole thing.

In retrospect this is ironic, since Jane now makes her living as an environmentalist.

Thus I still have hope for the men in my house – or at least, for Tyler and Joseph. The last time I tried to give Michael a conservation lecture, he was in the kitchen cooking with the refrigerator door wide open. I watched him shuttle from his cooking to the refrigerator and back, removing ingredients from the fridge and leaving the door open each time. I could practically *see* all the cold air pouring into the room. I kept getting up to close the door, and he kept leaving it open.

Finally he couldn't take it anymore. "SWEETIE, is it too much to ask that you leave the door open?! I'm cooking!"

"I REALIZE you're cooking! So why do you need the refrigerator door open to cook?!! You're a big strong guy – is it too much to open and close it when you need another ingredient?!!"

"Why does it matter?!!" he asked me with exasperation.

"WHAT??!!! To SAVE ENERGY!" I couldn't believe he had to ask.

"Sorry. I forgot." He handed me a plate. "Here sweetie, I made you a sandwich."

Oh.

I *was* pretty hungry.

Michael has always been good about fixing me food when he thinks I've forgotten to eat.

As I enjoyed my sandwich, I began to think

maybe I was being a little unreasonable about the refrigerator door thing. I can sometimes focus on the details and miss the big picture. In family life, it's hard to know who's putting up with whom.

A few wasted kilowatts are a little thing, next to the real power of Love.

Mike

For ten years, without fail, Ann and I kept our razors side by side in the shower. Then I switched to the Mach 3 triple blade razor, and suddenly the ever-present disposable pink lady razor disappeared. I didn't give it much thought at the time. I figured such a sissy razor was an embarrassment beside my macho marvel of modern technology.

The truth was more horrific. One morning I walked into the bathroom while Ann was in the shower, and I discovered that my Mach 3 triple blade marvel was being used to shave her legs. It didn't take much to surmise that it might be getting some time under her arms, too.

I kept my mouth shut until our morning coffee.

"Doesn't it repulse you," I said calmly, "to know that the razor you're using under your arms is the same one that I'm using on my face?"

Ann laughed, and then quickly reached for my hand. "Sometimes..." she replied with a serious voice. "But love is a strange and wonderful thing." She gave me an angelic smile.

All was forgiven.

Disagreement between a husband and wife occurs in the best of marriages. Sometimes this manifests as open argument. Other times, marital conflict can be more subtle, an unspoken tension permeating the relationship for years, like an uncomfortable humidity.

When I met Ann at that fraternity costume party, she was supposedly dressed as a Greek goddess, in a skimpy toga no father would have permitted his daughter to wear in public.

I fell in love.

After our three years apart, there was nothing I looked forward to more than marriage and spending my life with Ann. My attraction to her was more than just her physical beauty; I admired her talent, kindness, intelligence and discipline.

I still admire her. But after twenty-five years of marriage, the intelligence and discipline thing sometimes gets on my nerves.

Ann has tendencies towards frugality that do honor to her Scottish heritage. She also endeavors to be environmentally aware. These two qualities are evidenced in the temperature settings Ann prefers for the household thermostat. During the hot Georgia summer the air conditioning is set at 80. During the cold of winter the heat is set at 65. In January when I am cold, Ann tells me to put on a sweater. In July when I am hot, Ann tells me to take my sweater off.

Last year it was another hot, humid summer. So one day when Ann wasn't looking, I sneaked to the thermostat and deftly dropped the temperature five degrees.

It didn't take Ann long to notice. "Who turned the air conditioning so low, Michael?"

"Those kids," I responded, shaking my head disapprovingly. I was not lying. I was simply making a declarative statement designed to misdirect.

"The boys say they didn't touch the thermostat, Michael."

"Those kids," I repeated, shaking my head disapprovingly.

Ann laughed and moved the thermostat back to "where it belongs." I didn't argue. I could understand her perspective: why burn fossil fuels to lower the temperature of my house just so I could be a tad bit more comfortable?

But sometimes it was annoying. It was like I was married to Al Gore, and every time I touched the temperature control I was sinking an axe into the trunk of the last giant redwood.

Over the years, Ann had successfully colored our "thermostat decision" in spiritual terms. With artful language she conveyed to me sophisticated thoughts about the needs of the body versus the needs of the soul. Essentially, her argument boiled down to this:

Jesus didn't have air conditioning, so why don't you spend more time praying for strength, and less time whining about the heat?

One summer Ann left town to visit her sister for a week. It was like Dorothy's house had plopped down in Oz, and d*ing dong, you-know-who was dead!*

I ran to the thermostat like an unsupervised teenager and lowered it not five degrees, but ten. I was going to get all the air conditioning that compressor could muster. That night my house was so cold I needed another blanket from the closet. Immobilized by comforters, I slept like it was the dead of winter.

Condensation covered all my windows when I awoke. I shivered when I sat down to my morning coffee. Now *this* was what July in Georgia should feel like! I thought about getting out that dang sweater. Maybe I should light a fire too?

But after an hour of reflection, I simply turned the air conditioning off.

I missed Ann. Morning coffee was more fun with her. It's far better to have a home that is too hot in the summer and too cold in the winter than to suffer again through the fires and chills of a long distance relationship.

A prescription for tolerance is an occasional few

days apart. In our human struggles, we can sometimes fixate on small problems.

Absence gives God a chance to direct our focus on the big picture –

Love.

Mealtime

I'm having difficulty enough eating it; do I have to compliment it, too?

Ann

When Michael was a medical resident and Tyler just an infant, money was tight. I began stretching our grocery budget by serving rice and beans at dinner a few nights a week. Sharing this budget trick with Michael, I explained that it helped cover the diaper bills.

His eyes sparkled. "Why not rice and beans every night?' he enthused. "Just make a big pot - we'll have it for dinner. Think of all the money we'll save!"

With some reservations, I agreed. I'd sometimes found Michael a bit inconsistent in his whims. On the other hand, it was nice to receive approval for my efforts. Usually he was too tired to notice. That Sunday, I dutifully proceeded to cook up a large pot of rice and beans. Each successive evening, I spooned out a generous helping for dinner, along with the veggie sides.

On day six, Michael came home late. He'd worked fifteen hours straight in the E.R. at the hospital. As he slumped in his chair over his warmed-up dinner, he took one look at the rice and beans and threw down his fork in disgust.

"Rice and beans *again!!?*" He glared. "What do I look like - a third world country?!!"

Frankly, I was surprised he'd lasted this long.

It was no use reminding him it had been his idea; trying to feed an Italian a regimented diet should not be undertaken by the faint of heart.

For the *paisan,* food is a religion. Not one of those Puritan religions where you give thanks to God for skimpy plates of food, no matter how meager, but one of those religions where the grapes and wine are overflowing, and there's plenty of cholesterol and fat for everyone. When Michael was growing up, his dad Phil actually owned a business that made pasta, turning out exotic noodles with names like "tortellini" and "rigatoni." I'd been raised in the Midwest. We had spaghetti, of course, but when I was growing up, the only other pasta I'd heard of came from a can and said "Chef Boy-ar-dee."

Over the course of our marriage, Michael and I have sometimes tried cooking together, but so far we haven't found our "rhythm" in the kitchen. Our cooking styles reflect our personalities: Michael likes to experiment, in quantity, and be surprised; I prefer to follow recipes written by people who can cook.

We have reached an understanding. We're flexible in our everyday eating. But on special occasions with company, I cook the dinner.

And Michael eats it.

Mike

My doctor partners and I take turns being on call for the holidays: one of us has to be ready to run to the hospital if needed. Last year, my turn fell on Thanksgiving, but with no patient emergencies, I found myself, to my surprise, sitting down to the big dinner with my friends and family.

As I looked across the table at my loved ones and listened to their loud and animated conversation, I noticed they all seemed to be in various states of inebriation. I was not joining in the festivities of the fermented grape. No, I was on call and had responsibilities. After a while, I began to wish that the hospital would actually call me. Nothing is more annoying than being the only sober one at the dinner table.

Particularly when you paid for all the wine.

I sat at the table and thought about my unhappiness. The way I saw it, I had three choices.

One, I could make sure I wasn't on call the following year so I could join in the frivolity worry-free.

Two, I could cultivate new friends and family relations, ones less inclined to intoxicate themselves at holiday meals.

Or three, I could view this moment of unhappiness as a spiritual lesson and walk more strongly the path of Love, steadfastly refusing to experience unworthy, lesser emotions.

It was a no-brainer; I decided just not to be on call again.

Holidays are stressful, but particularly so for women. Women are more aware of the subtleties of celebration. They put effort into esthetic touches that would never dawn on a man. The intention, I believe, is to manifest beauty.

But occasionally the result is marital conflict instead.

Every Thanksgiving, Ann makes six dozen homemade crackers called "Cheddar Crisps." They come in three flavors: cracked blacked pepper, caraway seed, and something called nigella seed.

I never heard of nigella seed either; she orders it special online.

After watchfully monitoring the baking time and removing these handmade creations from the oven to cool, Ann carefully sequesters them in a tin box to be doled out at the proper moment. She serves them with a small bowl of homemade butternut squash soup - right after we say grace, and before we sit down for the main meal.

Every guest is given three crackers, one of each flavor. You feel yourself handling each one as though it's Great Grandma's favorite antique tea cup.

As far as crackers go, the Cheddar Crisps are delicious. Unfortunately, I am more a Ritz cracker kind of guy, accustomed to shoveling large quantities of whatever I am eating into my mouth until I am full. So for me, this cracker moment represents holiday stress. How do I express genuine appreciation for the work my wife has put into this pre-Thanksgiving snack, without conveying my true thoughts? *Stop wasting so much time already – they're just crackers!*

So I channel Effete Cracker Connoisseur and solemnly critique the subtleties of each flavor - how the steam from the soup opens up the palate so one can fully appreciate the differences.

The next year I finally got my wish. I was not on call, and there were no homemade crackers to be found!

I noticed a few things that surprised me.

Free to imbibe a glass of wine now that I wasn't working, I found I did not want any, but chose instead sparkling water. I also noticed that my holiday guests were not the sodden idiots inclined to boorish conversation that I remembered from the year before. They were actually beautiful people I am blessed to have in my life.

Perhaps the previous Thanksgiving I had been just a tad bit grumpy.

But the thing that surprised me most was that I actually missed Ann's homemade crackers.

It's not always easy for a man to appreciate the attention to detail an effortful woman brings into her family's life. Sometimes what she does seems frivolous. And God knows, sometimes it's expensive. But there is a reason for a woman's efforts, and this I understand – as a father, as a husband of twenty-five years, and also as a physician who has listened to so many of his extra effortful patients over the years...

A woman gives Life to her children, brings beauty to her home, and creates ties in her community. And wherever she goes, a woman will make Life more beautiful for us men –

Whether we want her to or not.

Home Decorating

Husbands know too little. And wives spend too much.

Ann

In decorating the house, including what colors we paint the walls, what furniture we purchase, and what accessories we display, Michael and I differ.

I notice. He doesn't.

By the time Michael and I had been married a year, I had begun to suspect that he was going to opt out of any decision-making in our home decor. Sometimes when I listened to him, I wasn't sure he and I were even living in the same home at all.

"Annie – can you hand me my glasses?'

"Where are they?"

"In the living room. On the cabinet."

"There's no cabinet in the living room."

"I mean in the dining room."

"There's no cabinet in here either."

"Umm, I mean up on top of the – what do you call it?"

"The hutch?"

"Right."

Once at Christmastime I conducted an experiment. It was Saturday morning. Strains of

Handel's *Messiah* wafted from the stereo as we drank our coffee, and Michael was alternating between reading the paper and talking to me. I sat down on the floor just to one side of him with two unwrapped gifts I'd purchased for him in plain view (a couple of shirts). I brought out the wrapping paper and ribbon. As Michael and I conversed, I placed the shirts into boxes and wrapped them. Michael continued to talk and look back and forth from me to his paper the entire time. I tied on the ribbons.

"There!" I said with a flourish, holding up the boxes.

"What?" he said.

"Those are a couple of your presents."

He looked at the gifts and then down at the floor, registering the paper scraps as the truth sank in. "Did you just wrap those in front of me?"

I stifled a giggle.

"Wow." He shook his head at himself. "That is just pathetic."

Mike

When Ann and I were newlyweds, I offered to help Ann pick out furniture for our apartment. In the course of shopping, I happened to voice a few rookie opinions.

"Eggplant" as a color name is a joke - right?

Ann appeared to conclude that I possessed no aptitude in the art of home decoration. She made it known that from then on, if she ever wanted my opinion, she would give it to me.

This goes for homes, too. After I finished my medical training, I told Ann I wanted to live in the country on a few acres. She told me she wanted to live in a subdivision.

So we compromised and moved to a subdivision.

I like the house Ann picked out. She lets me furnish it any way I want, with only a few stipulations. I can pick out anything I like so long as I keep it in my study. I must keep the door to my study closed.

These provisions have stolen my thunder just a little when it comes to decorating. Thus in the history of our marriage, I have purchased only two items of home decor: a First Edition issue of a Savage Sword of Conan comic book, which I had framed and double matted, and a World War I rifle. They are both in my study.

And yes, the door is closed.

A twenty-five-year-old hand-me-down couch which sat in our home office was actually my favorite piece of furniture. Ann kept it presentable with designer pillows and a canvas cover. Although not esthetic, the couch was comfortable. It was great to sleep on and perfect for wrestling matches.

Unfortunately, there was an unpleasant large round ottoman in front of the couch. On top of it Ann kept a wooden tray with two terra cotta Chinese warrior statues, whose heads broke off every other time the boys and I were roughhousing and accidentally knocked them over. I had glued the heads back on so many times the warriors looked like they had neck tumors.

Concealed under a skirt, the ottoman had four metal legs designed specifically for stubbing toes. Every time I hurt myself during a wrestling match, the boys lit up joyfully. The family cat joined in the fun by lurking under the skirt and taking swipes at me any chance he could.

I learned what an ottoman was the first time Ann and I went furniture shopping. As a novice home owner, I couldn't believe how expensive everything was. It stirred feelings of guilt long dormant when I started remembering my destructive childhood fights with Chris. Maybe I shouldn't have bashed him in the shins by toppling that Ethan Allen table.

Ann found a chair she loved with a price tag just outside our budget. I chivalrously hailed a harried salesman to make the purchase.

"You want the one with the Ottoman?" he asked me.

"Well," I hesitated, "I'm not really sure what *brand* it is. It's the white one over there."

The salesman looked perplexed.

Ann giggled. "An ottoman is a footstool, Michael – not a brand." She turned to the salesman. "He means the cream one, not the white." The salesman smirked knowingly.

This memory was yet another reason I didn't like that "*ottoman*" very much.

But one day when I came home, the ottoman was no longer there. I plopped down on my favorite couch, enjoying the extra space. I told Ann how happy I was that she'd finally disposed of that lousy ottoman.

There was a pregnant pause. Ann briskly informed me she was replacing my favorite hand-me-down couch with a custom-covered loveseat, which, although smaller and less comfortable, would "more proportionately address the bay window."

And - by the way - the missing ottoman was being reupholstered to match the loveseat.

As an experienced husband, I had long ago learned to recognize certain passing comments from Ann as signs of impending change.

Brass fixtures are so dated.

This wall covering is straight out of the 80's.

Our kitchen table doesn't properly frame the view in the dining area space.

But this time there had been no warning thunderclouds. I suppose the couch was ratty and should have been replaced years ago. But that lousy ottoman?

Conflicts arise in marriage because of different perspectives. Ann didn't understand why the boys and I wrestled on the furniture, breaking the heads off her dumb statues. I, in turn, didn't understand why the statues were there in the first place, teetering on an ottoman with a personal vendetta against my toes.

So I stewed on my twenty-five-year-old couch in silence. I didn't dare ask Ann how much she had spent. Any answer would only have made me feel worse.

Years later, I still miss my old couch. It was comfortable and inexpensive.

But, philosophically speaking, more important than the comfort of the body is the comfort of the soul. Healthy relationships are necessary for spiritual health. So... I guess I don't care how Ann decorates our home. Even when I do care.

When it comes to home décor, I have learned the most important element of all.

A happy wife.

Charming Idiosyncrasies
I remember when they were cute.

Ann

As soon as Michael and I moved in together, I saw that his living habits might present a challenge to marital harmony. Three nights in a row, I watched him drop his dirty socks directly on the closet floor, even though the hamper was yawning wide not six inches away.

I didn't want to nitpick, but I thought setting a few ground rules was important.

"Hey sweetie, can you just put your dirty clothes in the hamper?"

"Sure, I always do."

"Well, no, actually you're dropping them *next* to the hamper, not *in* the hamper."

"Are you serious?" He appeared genuinely confused.

Michael remembered my request the first night, and then promptly forgot the second. It dawned on me that my husband had just come out of a college apartment he'd been sharing with two other guys. Basic training might take a week. Maybe even two.

For several days, I continued unpacking,

assessing where best to place our respective personal belongings. As I observed Michael in his natural habitat of our apartment, I felt like a biologist taking field notes on the wildlife.

This was the towel rack he reached for when he came out of the shower. *This* was the bathroom sink he favored. *This* was the cloth napkin he always grabbed. And if I hung the shoe rack *here*, I had a 50% chance of him dropping his shoes underneath it.

You have to understand a husband in order to housebreak him.

"Subject steals pillows while asleep: Provide extra pillows."

Mike

I once heard an intelligent attorney express his understanding on the subject of women. His opinion could be called many things, but certainly neither "intelligent" nor "understanding." According to him, the reason men and women have difficulty relating is that women can't think rationally.

"Women are emotional," he proclaimed, one pedantic finger pointing skyward. "Women are not logical."

I found his comment deeply offensive. In the twenty-five years of our marriage, Ann has not done one illogical thing.

With one exception.

Or maybe two.

The boys have regularly complained about the uncomfortable pillows on my bed. There are big ones and medium ones and small ones. They are variously festooned with embroidery, or sequins, or knobby wooden beads, which makes them anything but comfortable. The assorted shapes and colors of these fifteen pillows require that they be painstakingly arranged, once the bed is made, in a precise array impossible for me to remember.

The boys suggested I get rid of them. Privately, I agreed. The purpose of a pillow is to provide something soft to snuggle – not something uncomfortable that increases one's everyday chores.

But Ann had a different idea. So instead of the "pillow talks" you might expect between husband and wife, Annie and I had pillow disputes. Sometimes they occurred on those rare occasions when I helped her make the bed and complained about the extra work. Sometimes the arguments arose when I was having trouble falling asleep and vented my frustration by flinging a few pillows on the floor, sequins notwithstanding.

In surgery there is an anatomical problem that requires repair. Surgery is logical: a purposeful action performed in an efficient, precise manner that directly impacts the welfare of another human being. Operating rooms are logical, too. You can look in every nook and cranny, and there is not one fancy pillow to be found.

"Why do we have so many lousy pillows that are impossible to arrange?" I'd ask rhetorically, my index finger pointing skyward. "It's not logical."

Sometimes my question made Ann laugh; sometimes it elicited an eye roll. But once in a while, she attempted to formulate an explanation for my edification. As an artist, Ann maintained that esthetically arranged visual elements uplift the spirit, imparting our mundane lives with a touch of the divine. Balancing the functionality of objects with an eye toward manifesting beauty is an act of meditation, even worship.

Mostly I ignored all this profound crap. A squabble was far more enjoyable.

But through the decades of my marriage and

practicing medicine, I have learned that sometimes it's best for a man to simply stand out of a woman's way.

What remarkable beauty you will see!

I remember Ann's cesarean sections in the O.R., the wondrous transformation of her frightened face when she heard our child cry for the first time. And I have witnessed thousands of times the miracle of a woman bringing new life into this world. I am in awe and wonder - and perhaps confusion, too, about the beauty of womanhood. Why would anyone sacrifice their body, blood and soul to usher into this world in an explosion of God's love a newborn baby?

It's simply not logical.

The Yard

I love yard work. I could sit and watch it for hours.

Ann

Michael and I don't see the same thing when we look at the yard. As an artist, I look outside and behold a leafy canvas to splash with colorful flowers and plants.

As a surgeon, Michael sees grass to be cut.

Preferably by someone else.

This actually works out well. I share yard duty with our longtime lawn guy. Between us, we take care of the lawn, the mulching, the shrubbery, and the gardening.

Michael's job is to come up with the compliments.

One fall day, after I had enthused about the satisfying exercise of raking a yard instead of blowing it, Michael's curiosity was piqued, and he ventured into the yard with a rake to help me. Our neighbor across the street, who had been chatting with us from the sidewalk, ran back into her house and emerged with a camera.

"What are you doing?" Michael asked.

"I'm taking a picture," she replied.

"WHY?" he asked, still confused.

"Well," she said, "you've been living across the street from me for twelve years. And this is the first time I've ever seen you working in your yard."

Mike

Sometimes our neighbors compliment me on having a nice-looking yard. I take no credit whatsoever. For ten years now, a local guy by the name of "Duffy" has been mowing and blowing my lawn. And Ann does the rest.

Ann regularly shares with me reports on her landscaping activities. She includes not only the details of her mulching, pruning, and digging, but also the Latin names for plants I have never heard of. I always nod my head politely. Since she's the one doing all the work, I figure it's the least I can do.

Recently the weekly news flash involved a Big Rock. Now, this Rock was minding its own business, buried in the ground between my neighbor's backyard and mine, half-covered with leaves and just barely sticking its nose into the air. Joseph stumbled upon it when he was walking through the woods and had the bright idea of digging it up. He discovered it was quite large and, knowing his mother's interest in all things obscure and natural, alerted her to his discovery. Ann proceeded to investigate.

It turns out this was no ordinary Rock. No, this was apparently a very attractive rock, a specimen of quartz, flecked with mica and other such minerals. Such a prize Rock should not remain underground.

No. A Rock like this should be dug up, heaved out of its hole, and moved a hundred feet into a prominent place in my backyard so we could all enjoy looking at it.

Mind you, I missed all the excitement because I was at work. Each evening I returned home to hear about the progress of Ann's Rock excavation and moving operation. Juicy details included how many shovels and 2" x 4" levers she had employed, what material makes the best ramps, and speculations about which section of the garden path would be best enhanced by this gem. Ann was clearly enjoying the challenge. She even went so far as to compare her efforts with those of the Egyptians, building the pyramids without power tools.

I didn't offer to help. My philosophy about yard work is that it's best to let sleeping rocks lie. Unfortunately, the Rock eventually proved to be too much of a challenge even for Ann. So it happened that when Saturday morning rolled around, just as I was settling down to read the morning paper, Ann requested my aid and manual labor in moving the Rock.

Saturday morning.

My aid.

Manual labor.

Now, I've been married twenty-five years. I knew I really didn't have a choice. But as I was stewing and finishing my coffee, I was also still trying my best to figure a way out of it. I began to consider grounding Joseph for making this discovery in the first place.

But then I remembered the one thing I ever

learned about big rocks.

A time management specialist was giving a demonstration. Into a large glass jar he placed a bunch of big rocks. He asked the audience how many of them thought the jar was full. Most raised their hands. Then he poured a bunch of pebbles into the jar, which filled the space between the rocks. Again, most watching considered the jar full. Then he poured in a bunch of sand and, again, most thought it full. Then he filled the jar with water.

He asked the class what the lesson of the demonstration was. One person raised his hand and said, no matter how busy you are, you can always fit in more.

No, that wasn't it. The point of the demonstration was this: Put your big rocks in first. Do what is most important in your life to get the most out of it.

So I got off my chair to help my wife.

I was hopeful the size of the Rock had been exaggerated. Nope, it was a big Rock, alright – two hundred pounds, easy. I spent the next half hour struggling to move it wherever Ann pointed. I was sore and grimy by the time the Rock was correctly positioned. But in the end, Ann giggled happily, cleverly *oohed* and *ahhed* over my biceps, and gave me a big hug.

Spending time with your spouse is a big Rock. It doesn't matter so much what you actually do. It's the together part that matters.

Sharing the Great Outdoors

Annie, my idea of "getting back to nature" is watching TV on the back deck.

Ann

The first year Michael and I were married, I planned an overnight camping trip for just the two of us to do some trout fishing in the mountain streams of north Georgia. I researched the locations of the best trails and trout streams and spent a few weeks day-dreaming a little about the nature experience we were about to share.

Unfortunately, I had failed to note that Georgia was in the grip of one of its worst droughts in twenty years. Michael and I ended up hiking along dry stream beds – no trout in sight – carrying on conversations by SHOUTING at each other because it was also a record-breaking year for the annual cicada hatching, and we could barely hear each other's voices above the din.

Michael said it was an even worse experience than when his mom sent him to survival camp in Ontario when he was thirteen, and he had to eat frogs and bugs for five days.

He pointed out that human beings had spent millions of years trying to conquer nature, and we finally succeeded. Why go back now?

Mike

A week after Ann joined the Georgia Native Plant Society, over ten years ago, we received an e-mail alarm. "Emergency - Plants in need of rescue." I was baffled. A Plant Rescue? Ann provided clarification.

The organization's rescue program endeavors to

"relocate native plants that are in the direct path of development." Volunteers dig up native specimens at prospective development sites, and transplant them to their gardens and to designated public park sites.

Excited about her first plant rescue, Ann set forth one early Saturday morning. Six hours later, she pulled back into our driveway, our brand new white minivan covered with mud. Ann was covered with mud, too, but she was in great spirits. Eagerly she opened the hatch to show me the cache of rescued plants she had brought home for our yard. "You will not believe all the great plants I found!"

Truthfully, I had been skeptical about the whole rescue thing. The image of a group of botanically-minded individuals combing the terrain for specific plant species a few days before the arrival of a bulldozer evoked images of eccentric professors traipsing through the jungle with butterfly nets. The emergency tenor of the e-mail struck my funny bone. Whenever the subject of the plant rescue came up, I hummed under my breath the various movie theme songs I associated with James Bond saving the day.

But Ann was expressing such delight I was now intrigued. What leafy marvels had she dug up? The sheer volume of mud covering both her and the minivan seemed to confirm the success of her mission. Perhaps there was something to this plant rescue after all! Why spend a fortune at the local garden store when we could dig them up for free? I felt guilty for mocking her; her botanical efforts would likely send my property value sky-rocketing!

Ann lifted the hatch with a flourish. The only items in sight were what appeared to be a half dozen or so grocery bags of dirt. No hundred-dollar tree. No fifty-dollar bush. Not even a ten-dollar fern.

"What do you mean, where are the plants?" Ann responded. "*These* are the plants," she said. She gestured again to the bags of dirt.

Had she found invisible plants? I leaned in to look closer and finally made out assorted bits of botanical matter that resembled sprigs of parsley. The truth was undeniable: Ann had spent the morning rescuing small weeds.

Ann's smile was fading fast in the face of my underwhelmed response. Quickly I changed gears and asked her to identify the species for me. She happily rattled off the common names of her treasures: Trout Lilies, Dwarf Crested Iris, Bloodroot, and my personal favorite - Sneeze Weed. Her momentum built, and to my credit I listened attentively to the entire lecture.

I must confess I lost interest well before she regaled me with the Latin names. But the gist is as follows: these are plants indigenous to Georgia that thrive in the forest understory beneath the canopy of tree branches. Most plants we install in our yards are not native to Georgia. Our lawns are anachronistic remnants from the days of the English Manor, and our lawn grasses and ornamental shrubs are not natural to this ecosystem. The problem has to do with the food web; native plants feed the insects, the insects feed the birds... blah, blah, blah...

It's the typical ecological scenario: the Hyenas have taken over the Pride Lands, the Circle of Life has been disrupted, and you and I are the Hyenas.

I find these environment diatribes particularly

vexing. And I refuse to lose sleep because some mosquito is low on Bloodroot.

Ann spent the afternoon preparing her flower beds under the trees and planting her rescued plants. She gave me a tour when she was done. It still wasn't too impressive; I had to get on my hands and knees to appreciate the tiny flowers she found so enthralling. But her efforts really made her happy, and she started drawing the flowers in her sketchbook. A concerned neighbor took me to the side the following week, delicately inquiring why Ann was spending so much time in our backyard staring at the ground.

Twenty years after the first rescue, our backyard is now populated with small native plants which continue to be difficult to see. For the boys and me, it has became a minefield: "CAREFUL! Watch out for the Milkweed!" Or, "PLEASE get off of the Liverwort."

But the Trout Lilies bloomed recently, and once again their small yellow flowers evoked such enthusiasm from Ann that her happiness was contagious.

I have made a disparaging comment or two over the years regarding Ann's native plant endeavors. But this year I found myself looking forward to springtime in my backyard and the return of small flowers.

God begins by teaching us tolerance. But if we look closely, He offers us also a gift. Through learning tolerance, we may gain at last something new –

A glimpse of the world through our loved one's eyes.

The Wild Kingdom

Mom, shooting paintball guns *is* a nature activity.

Ann

There are BB holes in my bird feeders.

Our back yard is wooded. For fifteen years I've been working to restore it to its natural state with native flowers and berries to attract birds and other wildlife. I see it as a mini-ecosystem.

Tyler and Joseph see it as a handy place for target practice.

Over the years, I have watched them run around with a pack of their fellow warriors dressed in masks, camouflage pants, and padded vests. At various times they have shot paintballs, airsoft pellets, arrows and BB's at a variety of targets pinned against my long-suffering trees.

I drew the line at BB holes in the feeder, and they lost their backyard privileges for a while. And their gun use, too.

The boys and I have learned to understand and appreciate each others' efforts. I applaud their aim when a particularly good shot ends up in the center of the bull's-eye (*Tyler, please move your target so you don't damage the native azalea*).

And they learned to notice the bugs, birds and berries that they sometimes have to wipe off their boots.

Mike

Light from the rising sun streaked in long beams across the backyard, highlighting a deer grazing not twenty yards from our house.

The boys and I moved our chairs to the kitchen window to better see. We watched the deer turn his head to munch on a nearby plant. He was so close we could see his black lips moving, the white hair inside his ears as they twitched. Ann was fixing breakfast. She asked what we were doing, and I motioned her over.

Ann took one look and shrieked.

"My hosta, my hosta!" She bounded out the back door, yelling and waving her arms. The deer leapt and ran into the woods.

Ann stomped back inside. She grabbed the milk and slammed the refrigerator door so hard the jars rattled.

Oops, I forgot. We don't like seeing deer in the backyard. They eat Ann's flowers.

Every few days Ann sprays a foul-smelling deer repellent on her most edible plants. Liquid "Fence" is made from putrescent egg solids and garlic. It makes my backyard smell like concentrated skunk urine. It's no surprise the deer mostly stay away.

I mostly stay away, too.

The boys loudly complained about what their mom had done. What's her problem? A large mammal that moves is a lot more interesting than plants that don't. *Hey, we have a right to enjoy nature, too.*

Their indignation was nonsense. The boys weren't appreciating nature – they were thinking how easy it would be to hit the deer in the butt with a slingshot. It was more likely that they were upset that another summer vacation had ended, and they had selected Ann as a convenient target for their early school morning grumpiness.

Why not attack their mother, the person who sacrificed her blood to give them life?

The four of us sat down to breakfast. Joseph was hunched over his bowl, shoveling cereal into his mouth. "My hosta, my hosta!" he muttered between slurps. "My poor, innocent hosta."

Tyler snickered. He cupped his hand over his mouth to intone in the hushed tones of a field guide: "The ferocious plant-eating deer has spotted his next victim. He moves closer to his prey. The hosta doesn't suspect. The deer bends down for the kill... closer... closer... there it is!! Aah, Nature is cruel. The hosta never really had a chance."

The kids were putting on a show, but the show on Ann's face was even better. Conflicting emotions played across her face – first the irritated gardener, then the defensive mother. Then she was laughing despite herself, and ultimately the affectionate mom won out. Her face relaxed into a smile. Attentive to the moods of her children, as always, Ann looked at the boys. "Well, I guess maybe I spoiled the 'nature moment' a little," she conceded.

Then, more plaintively, "I just wanted to enjoy the flowers this year."

It's true that the boys and I don't see Mother Nature as Annie does. For us it's just a big playground for our toys and games.

But a few days later, I noticed Joseph at the kitchen window, watching something with his binoculars. He suddenly ran to Annie's desk with the glasses and pulled her to the window. "Hey Mom – you need to look at this – it's a frog! See, on the edge of the pond?"

Ann peered through the binoculars. "I see it! Wow, that is so cool." Her face broke into a beautiful, radiant smile. "Joseph - thanks so much for showing me that.'"

Joseph looked a little self-conscious, but he smiled.

"Sure, Mom."

4

Brotherly Love

Ann   *Boys, there is no earthly reason
for you to be fighting.
God has been good to us in every way.
I insist on civil behavior,
no matter what your feelings are.*

Mike   That's right —
listen to your mom.
Go fight outside.

Battling Brothers

I do love him, Mom. There's no one I'd rather fight.

Ann

Tyler was two and a half when Michael and I gave him the good news that he would soon have a little brother.

"Tyler, Mommy is going to have a baby! You will be a BIG brother!! Wouldn't you like to have a little baby brother to play with?"

Tyler glared, and a thundercloud of displeasure cast its shadow over his round toddler face.

"No!" he proclaimed. "Just Mommy, and Daddy - and Tyler!!"

Tyler had no interest in play-acting with dolls and bottles to prepare for the upcoming Little Brother. After Joseph arrived, it only got worse. Michael and I took turns reassuring Tyler with extra attention - stacking blocks, playing wiffle ball in the yard, reading him extra bedtime stories. But every time we brought Joseph near, Tyler's mood took a nosedive. One morning when Joseph was sleeping nearby in his infant seat, Tyler noticed and scowled at his brother, tiny at two weeks. He began to emit a growl, low and rumbling.

My maternal alarm bells were shrieking. I tried to conceal my anxiety, scooping Tyler into my lap for a hug and reassuring him I loved him very much. He was distracted at this point - but I was unnerved.

"Annie," Michael explained, "Tyler is just like a wild animal. He feels the way he feels, he does what he does."

Michael insisted we not leave Joseph alone in the room with his big brother – until Joseph had grown big enough to defend himself.

It took three years.

Long Live the King.

Mike

Ann always seemed worried about our boys not getting along. Their constant antagonism kept her on edge. To me, it was just a normal part of being a boy and having a brother.

You have to fight someone.

When Chris and I were growing up, fist fights were common. Weapons, too, saw frequent use – slingshots, bows and arrows, BB guns...anything we could use to more effectively express our feelings for each other.

Once when we were twelve, our parents went out for the evening, leaving us two Swanson "Hungry Man" TV dinners, along with instructions regarding their preparation. What was *not* assigned was which twin got which dinner. When I opened the freezer, Chris standing close behind, he immediately claimed the Salisbury steak - it came with a chocolate cake dessert.

I was closer and was able to grab the steak for myself. An argument followed and escalated into a fight. When punches began to fly, I realized I was not going to be able to eat the chocolate cake unmolested. I told Chris if he wanted the cake so badly, he could *have* it! Wielding the frozen dinner tray in both hands, I clobbered him as hard as I could over the top of his head.

The blow was spectacular and knocked him to the ground. I tossed the shattered remains of the dinner next to him on the kitchen floor. "Enjoy it, you !&%@!" I left.

A few minutes passed. Oddly, Chris did not return to attack me. After a few more minutes, I began to get curious. Cautiously, I returned to see what he was up to. I found him groaning, still on the floor.

This scared me. In all our battles, I'd never seen Chris so hurt that he wouldn't get up to continue the fight.

"What happened?" he mumbled. He didn't know where he was! Trembling, I helped him to the couch, where he stumbled and collapsed. He was able to whisper just a few words. He wanted some water. I got him a drink of water. He wanted a blanket. I got him a blanket. He needed to eat. I cooked and served him the TV dinner – the one with the chocolate cake. He was still hungry; I served him my dinner, too.

"Please, Chris," I begged. "Are you okay? Are you okay?"

"I'm not going to make it," he croaked.

"I need to call Mom and Dad!"

"No, no... it's too late. Get me the Bible."

I ran to get the Bible. "What do you want me to read?"

He hesitated a moment. "Page 400," he answered.

Hands shaking, I began reading page 400 and stumbled through the words. I can't remember what passage it was, and in retrospect, it's obvious that

Chris couldn't have named a book, chapter and verse of the Bible if his life had depended on it. But at the time, I was too overwrought to notice.

Finally, Chris couldn't take it anymore. He started to laugh. And laugh. And laugh.

I was so relieved he wasn't going to die, I wasn't even mad.

Looking back, I think God must have put Chris and me in the same family for a good reason – even if it was only to teach us how to fight. Chris became an attorney, licensed to practice in New York, Georgia, and the Supreme Court. After all these years, he and I often have the chance to work together.

It's a relief to finally have him on my side.

Spiritual Siege

Michael, "we hate each other's guts" doesn't sound normal to me.

Ann

As Tyler got older, he and Joseph showed no signs of forging a truce. In fact, Tyler never seemed to miss a chance to fan the embers of brotherly conflict.

If Joseph ventured a comment in a family conversation, Tyler would shout him down. "Joseph, that's the dumbest thing I ever heard!"

When Joseph brought home an A from school, Tyler went on the attack. "That's so EASY! You should see the math I have to do!"

And even Joseph simply walking past would elicit Tyler saying with a shove, "Stay out of my way, Joey!"

There were weeks when Michael and I simply declared martial law for Tyler: "You are not to touch Joseph. You are not to say anything at all to Joseph."

When I thought of the hopes I'd had for my boys, I felt like I was watching something die. I'd grown up with my sister Jane as a constant companion. We'd played games, explored the neighboring farmlands, sung the same songs, and shared books. I had always pictured this kind of closeness for my children. Indeed, when Joseph was little, he had been ready to admire his impressive big brother and follow him anywhere.

But by the time he was four or five, Joseph had figured out that wasn't going to be an option.

Joseph fell back on his internal resources. He developed an impressive repertoire from the Little Brother Armory. This included annoying noises, getting his brother punished by playing the victim when either parent was around, and covert attacks on his older sibling's belongings likely to go unnoticed.

Michael said it was normal.

I was baffled. Michael and I made plenty of time to spend with each of them, reading at night, assisting with homework, cheering their games. There was plenty of room in the house, no food or other resources to fight over. There was no earthly need for rivalry.

I began to think of it as a spiritual struggle, with both Tyler and Joseph under siege.

One evening Joseph went into Tyler's room with a pushpin and poked holes through all the photos on Tyler's bulletin board - wherever Tyler's face appeared.

Tyler was frantic with outrage. "You better punish him!! Don't let him get away with this! He came into my room and *destroyed my property!!!*"

We corralled Joseph alone. "WHY did you do this?!" Just six years old, Joseph was confused himself. He could only answer, "I don't know." We grounded him for the damage, but in private, Michael was mostly just amused. He was happy Joseph was only poking holes in pictures and not in Tyler's face.

Sometimes I felt reassured by Michael's perspective. But most of the time, I felt an undercurrent of worry.

Mike

I didn't have to stretch far to understand Tyler and Joseph's relationship; my own childhood memories would serve. As a young father, I found the hardest part of the boys' fighting was reassuring Ann when she was wide awake in the middle of the night.

The Easter that Chris and I were ten years old, we each received a chocolate bunny. I thought I had never seen anything as amazing as my chocolate Easter bunny. With yellow and pink eyes made of candy, little whiskers carved in his chocolate face, and green cotton candy at his feet, my bunny looked alive, sitting up in the spun sugar grass. He even had a marshmallow bunny tail. He was much too nice to eat right away. I thought I might prop him up on my bedroom bookshelf to enjoy for a little while.

Chris took one look at his, ripped off the box top, and chomped off the ears.

For the remainder of the week I enjoyed looking at my bunny in his nest of edible grass. Finally I decided it was time. Slowly, reverently, I opened the box. I peered inside, and with a growing sense of horror saw that much of my bunny had disappeared! His back and the solid milk chocolate base had been methodically excavated in crescent-shaped, bite-sized pieces. And there was no marshmallow tail.

I had been robbed!! In rage and despair, I screamed for my mom.

Tearfully I showed her the bunny's tattered remains. Mom's brows came together in a familiar expression of anger, and she yelled for Chris. He came running into the room. A look of confused shock instantly appeared on his face. He vehemently denied any wrong doing and even offered up a few alternative theories. A manufacturing glitch at the chocolate factory? An ant problem? A hungry neighbor broke into Michael's bedroom?

Chris held up a few more minutes under Mom's furious cross-examination, but was finally sufficiently frightened into a confession. Yes, he had been biting off pieces of my bunny. Yes, he had left the face of the bunny intact so I wouldn't notice. Yes, he had taped the chocolate ears to the top of the box so my bunny wouldn't fall over once the base was gone. And yes, he had even eaten the marshmallow tail.

"But," he said, stressing the positive, "please notice both candy eyeballs are still in place."

Mom was livid. She leaped up to wag her finger in front of Chris's face.

How dare you take something that is not yours!
Stealing is wrong!
Gluttony is disgusting!
No punishment is enough for you!

Chris stared at his feet. Despite his best efforts, he was unable to fight back the tears. His shoulders heaved as he sobbed silently to himself.

"Do you understand what you did wrong, Chris?" Mom asked, her voice softening a bit. Chris nodded, head down, unable to speak. Tears streamed down his cheeks. Mom suggested he might want to apologize to me. Chris couldn't even get the words out.

Chris shuffled to his bedroom and collapsed on the bed. Even from the hallway I could hear him crying to himself. He was so obviously upset, Mom didn't spank or ground him. I think she was satisfied she had fulfilled her parental duties.

I had been looking forward to eating my Easter bunny, but I was stunned how ashamed Chris had become. I found I didn't even care about the taste of chocolate anymore.

A brother's suffering was even sweeter.

After Mom went downstairs, I felt quite chipper. I peeked into Chris's room, perhaps to savor his official apology, or maybe just to revel in his misery. He was still sobbing into his pillow, but sensing my presence, he looked up. Seeing me alone, he rubbed his eyes, sat up and walked over.

"About your bunny, Michael..." Chris's voice cracked. "I just have to say..." A smug smile crept over his face.

"It tasted SOOOOO GOOD!" He pantomimed chomping a bunny and, rubbing his stomach, began to laugh, just as he pushed me out of the room and locked the door.

Don't get me wrong. I got my brother Chris back many times in many other ways. But despite the years of fighting, we have ended up as friends.

When Tyler and Joseph fight, Ann and I level the playing field just as my mom did for Chris and me. Yet I can't help but think that Chris and I forged a bond of friendship - partly through fighting each other.

It's a brotherhood thing.

Playing Referee

Annie, they'll be out of the house in ten short years.

Ann

When Tyler was seven and Joseph four, we enrolled them in a martial arts class for tae kwon do. Michael wanted the boys to learn to defend themselves. Personally, I wasn't crazy about the idea of Tyler and Joseph learning more about how to fight. But the basic premise of tae kwon do appealed to me: once your child is truly confident in his fighting skills, he finds fighting unnecessary.

What Michael and I left unspoken was that the boys' most likely opponents would be each other.

Tyler and Joseph continued their training for years. Every Tuesday night after practice, we ate at the local pizza joint a few doors down from the training room, called the *dojo*. Sandwiched between the dojo and the pizza place was a comic book store where Pokemon cards were sold by the hundreds.

My boys were in paradise – all three of them.

For dinner Michael and I sat together on one side of the booth. The boys wiggled and kicked on the other side. To get rid of them before the pizza came, we fed them a steady stream of quarters for the video game machines.

It was great family time.

In channeling the boys' energy into martial arts, Michael maintained that where there were boys, there would be fighting. He also claimed it was a good idea to let them learn how to work it out on their own. That might be true, but I never felt comfortable with it. The finer points of when fighting was okay ultimately escaped me.

So when Michael was in the house, I left it to him to referee.

Mike

Every Halloween we set up a portable fire pit in our front yard and threw a party for the kids and parents who come by.

I looked forward to Halloween for two reasons.

First, because it was the one time of the year we got to talk to all our neighbors and see their children.

Most of the time our lives were so busy, it seemed as though we just waved to each other like polite strangers. But Halloween night, we usually drew a good crowd to drink hot cider around the fire, roasting hot dogs and marshmallows on long pointed sticks the boys and I had whittled the day before. Sometimes the kids got a little overenthusiastic in their cooking efforts. We learned the hard way to keep a fire extinguisher stowed beside the radio.

One year the last trick-or-treaters to arrive were two little sisters with sad faces. They appeared just after nine o'clock, chauffeured by a harried and exhausted-looking mom, still in a work uniform. Perhaps they had gotten a late start. I looked into their Halloween bags, which held only a few candies rattling around the bottom. It was the end of the night, and the trick-or-treaters had slowed to a trickle, so I took two unopened, five-pound bags of candy and dropped one into each trick-or-treat bag.

The smiles and giggles of those little girls made my day. Shortly thereafter, I went to bed. A few of our neighbors were still sitting by the fire drinking wine in our driveway. We just asked them to put out the fire when they left. They stayed until 2 a.m.: another successful party.

The second reason I looked forward to Halloween was the aftermath – that is, the candy left in the pantry. With Halloween, the Season of Overeating officially begins. One year, in a feeble attempt at abstinence, I put the leftover candy and marshmallows in a plastic bag and tied it tight, optimistically placing the bag high on the top shelf for "next" Halloween.

But when you come home after a long stressful day, leftover Halloween candies call to you like the Sirens called to Ulysses. "Eat me and feel better," they seem to sing. A few days after Halloween, I succumbed and made a small hole in the bottom of the plastic bag. I snuck a candy bar. Every day thereafter, I'd go to the shelf after work, reaching up to rustle under the marshmallows and pull out a Snickers, a Twix bar, or a Kit Kat. By my calculations, there were enough left to last me through the winter.

But one day, to my disappointment, I pulled out a Tootsie Roll. The next day it was the same. Curious, I pulled the bag down from the shelf. The small hole I had made was now a good deal larger. I pulled the marshmallows out; only Tootsie Rolls remained. My stash of good Halloween candy was gone!

The great thing about having children is that no

matter what the crime, you know exactly whom to blame. Using the tone of voice I reserve only for dire emergencies, I yelled for the boys, then ages eight and eleven. They came running. Without saying a word, I showed them the remaining contents of the candy bag.

Their responses were what you would expect: denial, and denial. They looked at each other in feigned confusion. *What happened to Dad's candy?!! I know it was Joseph, Dad – I saw a bunch of extra wrappers under his bed! DAD - it was Tyler!! I can't even REACH that high!!* I listened to their protests in growing anger. I was stressed from work. I needed relief. Where was my candy?

I fell back on our well-rehearsed tae kwon do routines and barked out the Korean command for attention: "cheer-iot!" From habit, Tyler and Joseph snapped to attention, standing ramrod straight with their arms at their sides.

At moments like these, the true value of those expensive martial arts lessons becomes apparent.

I looked them over. What punishment, I wondered, would fit the crime? Oscar Wilde said it best when he quipped, "Never hit a child – except in anger." I never hit my kids. It's not because I didn't want to – I was just afraid if I start hitting them, I wouldn't be able to stop.

But this time would be the exception. Taking a deep breath, I whacked Tyler on his head - with a bag of marshmallows. Then I turned and whacked Joseph. And then, just as I had always feared, I couldn't stop. *Whack! Whack! Whack!*

But after a few whacks, Joseph executed a deft

move and skillfully blocked the marshmallow bag, and then, with some ancient Korean wisdom living on through the centuries, was able to grab the bag from my hand and counterattack.

The bag burst open. There were marshmallows everywhere.

I glanced at Ann, standing behind the kitchen counter making dinner. I was concerned she would be annoyed by our antics, but she was pointedly ignoring the ruckus. So the boys and I began to *really* fight.

Marshmallows, when thrown with sufficient velocity, can sting. The next five minutes brought on a marshmallow free-for-all.

Just before dinner, we stopped and cleaned up our mess. We were laughing and arguing about who got in the best shots. I never realized leftover Halloween candy could be so much fun.

Our lives are stressful and, sometimes, too busy. We wave to our neighbors without speaking. We eat without enjoyment. We discipline our children without understanding the cause of their behavior.

God often surprises us with simple solutions just under our noses -

Like bashing our misbehaving children with marshmallows.

Taking Sides

How can I have a favorite when you both drive me crazy?

Ann

The winter that Tyler and Joseph were eleven and eight, Michael had to work during the boys' winter break. I was staying home with the boys. In a burst of optimism, I planned on a few quiet afternoons with just the three of us eating popcorn, watching movies, and playing board games.

On the first gray day, I broke out the Monopoly board after lunch and called the boys to the game table. As a precautionary measure, I appointed myself the banker - so we could eliminate any conflict.

I would call this another example of maternal optimism.

Joseph's first roll landed him on "Community Chest," where he drew the card, "YOU INHERIT $100." I was about to hand him his money when Tyler, who had been watching his brother intently, let out a yell.

"You cheated, Joseph!! I saw you! You drew the second card, not the one on top!!"

"I did NOT cheat!!"

"Look, Mom – you see? The one on the top has a fold in it!! It says 'GO TO JAIL!' That was supposed to be Joseph's card!! Joseph took the one underneath!!"

I stopped to look at Tyler. Suddenly I was suspicious. "Why does the 'Jail' card have a fold in it?"

Tyler assiduously ignored my question. "Joseph cheated!! I'm not going to play with a cheater!!"

"Joseph, did you take the second card, not the first one?"

Joseph was already pouting. "I'm not playing! I don't want to play with a JERK!!!"

"You cheated!!"

"You set me up!!"

"MOM!!!" From both of them.

After intense negotiations, I got them back to the table for a few more casts of the die, with a promise from both to "play fair." But in the end, I surrendered the game in the midst of another squabble, and I sent them to their rooms for the rest of the afternoon. They each got to hear my stock lecture about playing by the rules and keeping high standards.

I've always figured one more lecture on right and wrong can't hurt them.

Michael called it "planting seeds in barren ground."

Mike

I've never been accused of being hypocritical. But when Tyler turned thirteen, I discovered to my surprise that I was.

DAD, I think you are being EXTREMELY hypocritical! EXTREMELY hypocritical!

Tyler's accusation caught me off guard. He was glaring at me.

"Tyler," I asked with an attempt at mildness, "is this really an example of *EXTREME* hypocrisy? Couldn't it just be the *flavor* of hypocrisy?"

Tyler smiled but quickly regained his indignant expression. No, he assured me, the adjective he had chosen fit the situation very well.

Tyler and I had been playing on the computer all morning. Then Joseph arrived. I included him in the game. An argument erupted. I don't remember the details - typical shouting and name-calling. I became annoyed. I chased Tyler away and let his younger brother stay.

Tyler now angrily reminded me that a few weeks earlier a similar situation had arisen. Only *that* time I had been playing on the computer with Joseph. When Tyler had arrived and an argument had ensued, I had let *Joseph* stay and chased *Tyler* away!

"And that's why I call you EXTREMELY hypocritical, Dad!" Tyler's nostrils flared. "EXTREMELY!"

I plopped down on Tyler's bed and grabbed an extra pillow to prop up my head. Tyler glared at me, his eyebrows furrowed to broadcast the message, *how dare you lie on my bed?* But I wanted to be comfortable. And this one would take a few minutes to digest.

Silence descended. Tyler began reading a book, ignoring my presence. I grabbed one of his comic books and leafed through it.

"Your bed is so comfortable, Tyler," I said. "I could lie here for hours. Could you just go downstairs and get me a glass of ice water?"

Tyler laughed despite himself. "I'm not getting you *anything*, Dad." Silence overtook us again.

I thought about the relationship between my sons over the past decade. Being an OB-GYN, I have seen many children excited about their mother's pregnancy, the prospect of a younger sibling. In the exam room, they grow wide-eyed with wonder, listening to the sound of the heartbeat of their unborn brother or sister.

Not so in the Litrel family. Tyler was three years old when Ann became pregnant with Joseph. Tyler was not excited about the arrival of Joseph, nor were his eyes full of wonder.

He was outraged.

After Tyler's growling incident with his newborn brother, Ann and I didn't leave Joseph alone with him at any time while Joseph was an infant. Baby birds will sometimes push a sibling out of the nest, and I didn't want to find out what human siblings might do.

I was still protective of Joseph, so Tyler's complaint was accurate.

But that doesn't mean I played favorites. I was careful not to let Joseph manipulate me. I had the answer ready when he tried.

Daddy, why did Tyler get two pieces of candy, and I only got one?

"Joseph, that's because I love Tyler twice as much as I love you."

It was always good for a laugh, only because Joseph knew I was joking. I reassured them often how much I loved them and what they meant to me. Deep emotions of love have to do with God and life's meaning and our purpose here on Earth. The ideas are difficult to put into words - but it's worth trying, anyway.

Kids understand better than we think they do.

Tyler was still sulking, an angry scowl on his mug. I fell back on my time-tested defense.

"Tyler," I said earnestly, "I don't think in this instance I'm being hypocritical. I just love Joseph more than I love you."

Tyler laughed. A few minutes passed. "Okay," he said begrudgingly, "maybe you're not a hypocrite. You're just playing favorites."

Then we got back on the computer together, just he and I.

Civilized Behavior

You boys can join us when you're more mature.
Like in 20 years.

Ann

The autumn that the boys were nine and twelve, we took a family vacation to Canada. One morning we set out to explore downtown Toronto on foot. Joseph insisted on leading the way.

"Dad, give me the map – I'll navigate. I'm good at this," he said with assurance.

Twenty minutes later it was evident we were lost. The sun was getting hot. "Joey, you got us lost!" Tyler fumed. "You're not Sacajaweya – You're SUCKY-Joe-wee-yah!"

An argument followed.

The problem with being lost on family vacations is mainly this: there's no place to put your kids in time out. We continued to listen to the boys bicker, until we came upon an outdoor café. Conveniently, it was right next door to the city police station.

Michael flagged me for a brief conference: we were in agreement.

He pulled first Tyler, then Joseph, to opposite

ends of the large police station sign. The boys were slouching twenty feet from the nearest café table. Michael and I sat down and proceeded to enjoy a leisurely meal with Tyler and Joseph in plain sight, but out of earshot.

We have a memorable photograph from this vacation of the two of them sulking in front of the large City of Toronto Police sign.

In later years, Michael used a variation of this incident as a technique to bring the boys' fights to a close. He would ground them both to their bedrooms until they could demonstrate civilized behavior, and be "best of friends."

Mike

Growing up, Chris and I each had a dog. Linus was mine, Valentine was Chris's, and they didn't like each other very much. Like their masters, Linus and Valentine fought each other furiously and often. They were big dogs with bigger teeth, and the best way to break up their fights was to blast them with a garden hose. That way, you got to keep all your fingers.

Our boys often reminded me of dogs who don't like each other. Arguments on family car rides were the most annoying, reaching a new low one day when the boys chose to do battle over a pair of old socks.

"HEY!" Tyler barked and turned on Joseph as we left. "DON'T wear my socks, you loser!"

"I didn't - you JERK!"

"You did too! And I'm NOT taking care of them!"

Tyler threw the socks at Joseph. Joseph became furious. And just like that, there was a dog fight in my car. There's never a garden hose around when you need one. The ride to the store was less than two miles. But even a five-minute drive is long enough to put a damper on a nice evening.

It didn't make me happy when my kids fought. But they did, no matter what I said or what consequence I imposed. Sometimes I wanted to beat the tar out of both of them. But I worried it might be hypocritical to pound my kids because they were pounding each other.

When at last we got home and out of the car, I made my pronouncement: "YOU ARE BOTH GROUNDED. YOU WILL STAY IN YOUR ROOMS UNTIL YOU ROT! OR UNTIL YOU LOVE EACH OTHER – DEEPLY!"

This was a tongue-in-cheek proposition. I would have settled for just a little civil behavior. But I just wanted them away from me so I could have some peace. I wanted a happy family – not the one that I was experiencing.

So I sat downstairs in the recliner with a book and a glass of wine, examining my parenting performance. I aspired to live a peaceful, loving life, not to lose my cool. I pined for the good ol' days, when a garden hose worked so well.

But this time, an hour's cooling off worked a minor miracle. The boys appeared before me, with their arms around each other, smiling broadly.

"Look how much we love each other, Dad!"

I noticed Joseph digging his knuckles into Tyler's ribs and Tyler choking Joseph in return. Both were wincing. But they were laughing at the same time.

This was good enough for me.

Family life had changed as the kids got older. When the boys were little, I'd walk through the front door after a long day at work and they'd launch into my arms, shouting *Daddy, Daddy!*, their faces lit with incandescent joy. Those early years of parenting were a challenge, but the outpouring of my children's young love was so palpable, I found it painful being away from them.

But as soon as they became teenagers, it was painful to be around them.

Forget about the pitter-patter of little feet greeting me at the door. As teens, Tyler and Joseph were often ensconced in the basement watching television or surfing the web. If I walked downstairs, I might score a salutary grunt. But if they were engaged in an online game with friends, their greeting could teeter on a glare.

One night, I was surprised to arrive home and find my boys once again greeting me at the door. Their teenage faces, however, were alight not with the childhood joy I recalled, but with adolescent anger.

There had been an argument, and they wanted me to arbitrate.

The last thing I wanted to hear at the end of a day in the operating room was a pile of teenage crap. I scanned their faces and briefly considered falling back on my father's casual approach to parental mediation. "I think you boys just need to take your argument outside."

When I was young, my father focused his parental efforts on preventing damage to the walls and furniture. As a boy, I found that nothing gave me more satisfaction than giving Chris a bloody nose. First, the success of firm contact... followed by an immediate cry of agony... and finally, blood, pouring miraculously between his fingers as he held his nose.

From a boy's perspective, it was like a hug from

Heaven.

It seemed an eloquent way to tell my brother exactly how I felt about him – serving equally well to warn him not to mess with me in the future. My father's parenting style, combined with a dozen years of martial arts training, eventually made Chris and me pretty good fighters. But I have a few scars as reminders of times that Chris got the upper hand.

In this case, unfortunately, my father's "take it outside, boys" strategy wouldn't work. Tyler was three years older than Joseph and a foot taller. Tyler actually bragged about his restraint following their verbal altercations. "You should be rewarding me, Dad," he would argue. "Joey *deserves* to be hit, and I *don't!*"

On this occasion, Tyler spouted out his complaints first. Joseph had hacked into one of Tyler's computer accounts to play the game without his permission. Adding insult to injury, Joseph had changed the password to one of his own choosing: "tylerisajerk."

Joseph rebutted that Tyler hadn't played the game in over a year, and no matter how politely he had begged, Tyler had refused Joseph access. Tyler deserved not only the hacking of his account, but also his new password.

As I listened to the complaints, my mind wandered. I couldn't help but think, *I could be relaxing right now – if only Tyler had let his brother play in the first place. Joseph was wrong, of course - but on the other hand, the password replacement was sort of slick.*

Years ago, I'd learned it didn't matter what I decided. One of the boys was going to end up angry and indignant. I just wanted a peaceful home. So in a test of my dad's parenting wisdom, I kicked the boys outside until dark. No admittance for either one until they made up.

An air of peace and calm descended over the house. I could breathe more easily.

A few hours later, Tyler and Joseph returned. After a long walk together through the neighboring woods and down to the lake, they said they could assure me they were now the very best of friends.

I was skeptical. I requested to see a convincing brotherly handshake. They were laughing as each strained to crush the other's hand, in what could only be called a somewhat aggressive hand clasp.

I took a photo of their smiling faces on my cell phone to add to my collection. They retreated to the basement to play videos. I stared with amusement at their picture for a few more minutes.

Who would have thought? All these years I'd been wrong.

"Take it outside, boys" was a strategy that really worked.

Reconciliation

Underneath all that fighting - a friendship?

Ann

Throughout the years, Tyler had always insisted he was a good big brother to Joseph. The proof he produced was not exactly heartwarming.

"I never, NEVER hit him - even when I really want to!!"

When I reflected on the boys' relationship, I couldn't help but feel the shadow of something wrong in our family. I felt I was in mourning over what could have been.

As Tyler neared the end of his high school years, he seemed to lose interest in attacking his fraternal nemesis. An uneasy truce reigned in the household. Every once in a while, Joseph would even mention some nugget of advice Tyler had given him at some moment I had not witnessed - how to deal with a particularly bad teacher, or the best way to blow off a bully.

I began to think that perhaps brotherly love has some mysterious spiritual dimension, a Presence not detectable by the mere mortal mother's eye.

It was August. Tyler was eighteen, making

preparations to leave home for college. Curious about this upcoming transition, I approached Joseph when he was sitting alone.

"So, do you think it will be kind of a relief when Tyler is gone? You know, a little more space in the house?" I wanted to go ahead and say it for him, so it would be easier for him to voice his feelings - no matter how hard for me to hear.

"What?" he looked up. I tried to keep my facial expression neutral.

"Do you think you'll miss Tyler a little, or maybe just feel relieved when he is gone?" I prompted.

Joseph, the little one, the scrappy survivor with his endless annoying defenses, the undisputed target for years of his brother's pushes and put-downs, pulled off his earphones and looked at me.

"MOM, I'm going to miss Tyler A LOT!!" A fleeting expression of sadness crossed his face, quickly replaced by a look of mild annoyance.

"I mean - he's my BROTHER."

5

Growing Up

Ann

Let's agree
we want the boys to learn
good values
that will guide them all their lives.

Mike

Annie,
the main value
I want them to learn
is leaving my house
when they turn eighteen.

Responsibility and Family Pets
How was I supposed to know the tail comes off?

Ann

Michael and I had always agreed we were "dog people." We would never consider a cat for a family pet. So I received a shock one Christmas Eve when Michael walked into the house with a cat from the local animal shelter.

Michael explained it was a surprise gift for Mary, who has always had a soft spot for animals, even Asbestos (Bastet). Michael's rescue was an appealing brown tabby with a running purr like a motor. He would make a great companion for Mary's Bastet. I gave him a few strokes as I admired my husband's thoughtfulness. After breakfast the next morning, Michael left the house to make his special delivery.

He returned less than an hour later. *With* the cat.

Michael said Phil had taken one look at the cat and, despite Mary's pleas, had refused to allow another cranky, hair-shedding feline into his house. Michael shook his head and looked at me ruefully. "Um, Annie – should we take him back to the shelter?"

Inwardly, I groaned. Tyler, eleven years old and

wary, remained noncommittal. But eight-year-old Joseph was instantly at my side, pulling on my sleeve. "Can't we keep him – PUHLEEZE, Mom?!!" His brown eyes were wide and serious as he solemnly pledged to take care of the cat "every day."

I was trapped.

Mary named the cat "Horus," after the Egyptian sky god, to go with her "Bastet." Michael and I waxed optimistic about the life lessons awaiting the boys as they learned responsibility and empathy from caring for our new family pet. We extracted promises - from Joseph, at least – that he would feed the cat every day. If he was neglectful - well, Horus was headed straight back to the shelter.

A week passed. Reminders to feed the cat were increasingly ignored. The laundry room began to smell from unchanged kitty litter. Another week went by, and parental hectoring and nagging reached a fever pitch, with the boys finally declaring they were not, and never had been, interested. Three weeks after Horus' arrival, Michael and I were forced to take action.

We kicked Horus into the backyard, propped open the screen porch door - and let him stay.

With admirable speed, Horus adapted to his new environment. Supplementing his dish of dry cat food, he began honing his hunting skills on the small birds, lizards and chipmunks I had so carefully nurtured with my "nature restoration" efforts in the yard. Horus became a walking, stalking conservation disaster.

Now Michael and I didn't have a conflict over the litter box. The question had shifted from "Who's cleaning the litter box?" to "Who's taking out the dead chipmunk?"

Since then, seven years have passed, and in hindsight, it's clear that having a family pet has indeed provided some great lessons.

Just not for the kids.

Michael has learned to feed the cat, to brush Horus when he lies down beside him on the arm of the easy chair, and to get up to let him in and out whenever he meows at the door, at all hours of day or night.

And I have learned to have empathy. I can't stand the effect Horus has had on my backyard wildlife. Nevertheless, when he lays his innocent hunting trophies at my feet, as he periodically does, I can almost see how proud he is, and I remind myself to close my eyes and take a deep breath.

Horus can't help it that God made him the Great Backyard Hunter, and I can't help it that God made me the Reluctant Cat Owner.

Mike

When Tyler and Joseph were five and eight years old, they begged us for a dog. I knew what a dog would get us: work, strife, messes, and nagging. I needed to come up with an alternative. After a visit to the pet store, inspiration struck: I would buy them each a pet rat.

Annie was skeptical. I explained my rationale. Rats were great "practice" pets, the perfect warm-up for the inevitable family dog in a couple of years. Contrary to popular belief, I expounded, rats are cute, intelligent, social, and clean. They don't require housetraining, can learn to answer to their name, and can live contentedly in a small tank or cage.

And the best part: unlike a dog or a cat, they only live about two years.

The entire pet experience - excitement, companionship, responsibility, boredom, resentment, and grief - all rolled into 700 days.

A week before Christmas, I told Tyler and Joseph that I had spent only eight dollars on their presents, but that they would absolutely love them. Intrigued, they spent the next seven days speculating and begging unsuccessfully for hints. On Christmas morning, after Santa's loot had been unveiled, I ran to get the rats, secreted in a hidden tank. Thrusting them with difficulty into a gift bag, I sat the boys together and deposited the package in their laps. Cautiously, they peered inside.

A large black and white rat crawled out of the bag and onto Tyler's shoulder. A look of mingled surprise and terror flashed on his face before he lit up. "Aw, Dad, you got me a rat," Tyler said, smiling ear to ear. "You are so cool."

That comment alone was worth the eight dollars.

I soon discovered, however, that there were some hidden costs in rat ownership.

Every day, as our rat manual instructed, the kids took the rats out of their tank and played with them for an hour. Joseph's rat, "Peaches," was easy to handle, but "Crookshanks" was soon re-christened "Chompers," after an incident in which he mistook Tyler's chocolate-smeared finger for a candy bar and took an exploratory bite. Once the crying and screaming subsided, we belatedly consulted the manual and learned that washing one's hands is imperative before handling these well-meaning but sharp-toothed creatures. Rats have a remarkable sense of smell – but they are a little near-sighted.

The play hour led to problems. Rats like to hide – under the sofa, inside the stereo speaker - the more obscure the hiding place, the better. So we established a system: keep the rats in an enclosed and easily cleaned area in the basement.

One day a few weeks later, ground rules in place, the boys and a friend were playing with the rats in the basement. As I sat by the fire with a good book, I could hear muffled laughter, crying, and yelling. But the shouting never reached the decibel level that required I leave my recliner.

The kids came upstairs, red-faced and sweaty, carrying sundry items and wearing big smiles. I looked over at the tank. Only one rat was inside.

Where is Peaches?

We couldn't find Peaches.

What do you mean, you couldn't find Peaches?

No response. Three sets of shoulders shrugging.

During the next hour, I led the boys on a reconnaissance to recover Peaches. My leadership style was not one of aplomb and dignity. The "enclosed rat play area" had been left wide open. Every time I discovered a new escape route, I shrieked in anger. Peaches could be under the television! Peaches could be inside the closet! Peaches could be behind the walls!

I was experiencing flashbacks. Thirty years ago I had accidentally let my brother's hamster escape. He had crawled under the heater and could not be coaxed out. Three days later, I found him dead on the floor.

I did not want *two* dead rodents on my conscience.

At last we heard chewing noises from the closet. It took ten minutes to remove enough toys and blankets to unearth Peaches. The rat was trembling in a corner. When I reached to pick her up, she tried to bite me. Why was she so frightened?

A reluctant confession followed. Maybe Peaches

became frightened during the pillow fight? In a flash, it all became clear – unsupervised, rambunctious boys stomping around and socking each other, all the while unintentionally terrifying the small, near-sighted mammals under their care.

My quiet evening was ruined. As I went for Peaches, I searched my mind for ways to ruin my boys' evening, too – I mean, to teach my children consequences and responsibility. Wary of Peaches' teeth, I snagged her by the tail. She thrashed around frantically as I took her to her cage.

A lizard's tail, I know, will sometimes break off - as a survival mechanism, if something catches it. But I never knew that the same goes for rats, until the moment Peaches hit the ground running, and I found myself still holding the appendage that used to be the tip of her tail.

Fifteen minutes later I finally caught Peaches. I put some antibiotic ointment on her injury and returned her to the tank.

Joseph was upset, of course. He began crying, sobs racking his small body. "I have a question, Daddy," Joseph sniffed, fighting to control his emotions as he looked at Peaches in the tank.

I knew what Joseph was going to ask me. He wanted to know if Peaches would die. I didn't think so - but then again, I didn't know much about rats. I felt a mixture of guilt and remorse from hurting his rat and not supervising the boys - and annoyance the boys hadn't been more conscientious. This was one of those childhood - and parental - pet lessons. You bear responsibility for another life, for a creature that needs your help to survive. You suffer grief when you fall short.

My son struggled to put his question into words. The moment seemed to go on forever. I wondered how the mind of a six-year-old boy would frame such an existential question. I waited patiently. Joseph finally stopped sobbing and spoke, his voice high and quavering.

"Can I take Peaches' tail to Show and Tell?"

Hmm. A bit different from the question I had expected. I paused a moment to assess the request, and then acquiesced. We put the tip of the tail in a plastic bag, and we took a photo of Peaches' freshly medicated injury.

The next day, I asked Joseph how Show and Tell had gone. He looked down at his feet. Didn't your friends like it? Well, the boys loved it. But the girls and his teacher - they were grossed out.

Joseph looked up at me and smiled mischievously. "Really, really grossed out, Dad!"

Motivating the Kids
It would be easier just to beat them.

Ann

Tyler's fourth grade year was rough on all of us. He was miserable in school, and sometimes he managed to make the rest of us miserable, too.

Michael and I wondered if home schooling might be a good change of pace. In a sober year-end conference, his excellent teacher tactfully admitted that Tyler was a tough one and that homeschooling "might be worth a try."

When I was younger, I'd been a good student with a natural tendency to help my fellow classmates. I didn't think to doubt my ability to give Tyler a quality home schooling experience. I dug into a stack of teacher's guides, textbooks and curriculum outlines. This was going to be fun!

Unfortunately, I was not the student.

No matter how enthusiastic I was or how hard I tried, I couldn't get Tyler to pay attention. One day I took him on a field trip to Atlanta's Michael C. Carlos Museum with its world-class collection of antiquities, including a few real mummies. In preparation, I had worked late the night before, poring over the museum website to design an exciting "scavenger hunt through the ages."

In the morning when we entered the museum, I unfurled my colorful chart with a sense of satisfaction. I was optimistic that Tyler would finally receive the learning experience he needed to transform him from boorish ten-year-old to inquisitive scholar.

Tyler was singularly unimpressed.

With scarcely a glance at the thousand-year-old vases and only a slightly longer pause before the ancient weapons and mummy bones, he finished the museum tour in record time. At the end, he turned to my scavenger list and sighed.

"Okay, let's just get this over with."

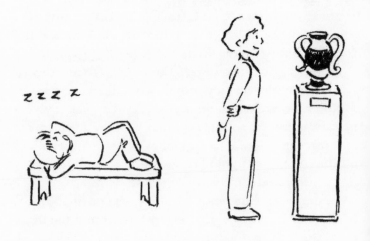

Mike

When Chris and I were growing up, Mom sometimes referred to us as her "house apes."

I don't think the expression made a huge impression on me at the time, but I began to more fully grasp her meaning once I had a couple of house apes living with me.

When Tyler was ten, I noticed that he was using my computer for his schoolwork; the telltale sign was the keys sticking to my hands. At that point, Tyler's attitude toward school had evolved into the one that would follow him for the rest of his educational career through high school: he did not enjoy school.

His teachers began to notice. And so did I. Ann met with the responsive, concerned staff and discussed with them possible reasons for Tyler's behavior. ADHD? Poor attitude? Laziness?

Yes, yes, and yes. But these are all part of the larger syndrome of being a house ape – that is, a normal ten-year-old boy.

One weekend, Tyler, during a typical house ape tantrum, threw an orange on the floor. Then he lay face down on the hardwood and pounded his hands and feet - just like you see in the old cartoons. He was upset about a report that was due. The subject of the report was supposed to be "Our Family History."

I suspect if I had been forced to write about this particular topic, I'd have thrown a temper tantrum, too.

Ann is the mature one in our marriage, and for that I am grateful. She told me to leave Tyler alone, that she would manage him with "good communication and acknowledgment."

Now, it's true that Ann knows quite a bit about communication and all, but she doesn't know one thing about how to handle house apes. So as soon as she went upstairs - to pray, meditate, or hide, I don't know which - I grabbed Tyler by the ear and threw him in the bathroom so he could throw his tantrum in a way that didn't disturb anyone else.

Why the bathroom?

When Ann was pregnant, my father bought us a baby shower present, a series of tapes on good parenting. I found the gesture a bit ironic. My recollection of my father's parenting was that he had mainly used the classic Two-Step Technique. The first step was to tell the child to "get the stick."

The second step was to take the stick and beat the child's bottom.

Anyway, I don't remember much from the parenting tapes, but one valuable tip I did glean was that the bathroom is the most boring room in the house. When your child is behaving badly, the bathroom is the perfect place for a "time out." I loved the concept. It seemed so civilized - lock the child away somewhere so you can't beat his fanny.

So I put Tyler into "bathroom time out." This caused an outbreak of Tyler yelling, accompanied by some well-placed kicks on the walls of the bathroom. Ann was still upstairs, presumably trying to regain her sanity. I opened the bathroom door like an enraged wild man and proceeded to shout at Tyler just like my father used to shout at me. Tyler's eyes widened. I demanded he follow me into the basement. I told him he was "in for it."

"*No Dad, please Dad, I'm sorry Dad,*" Tyler pleaded. He was genuinely frightened. Witnessing his fear brought back memories of when I was ten. I used to be scared, too.

"It's too late for that - now you are going to get it!" Looking in Tyler's eyes, I could see the wheels turning as he tried to guess what "it" was. Then I took him firmly by the shoulders and propelled him across the floor to the treadmill. I cranked the incline to its steepest.

"You will run at any pace you choose for a full thirty minutes." Tyler stared at me.

School was tough for me, too. They didn't have the fanciful diagnosis ADHD back then, or all the drugs that dull the symptoms and make it easier to control kids. But I hated school, just like Tyler. All that school work, when you just want to be outside with your friends having fun. *Fun* – it's what makes a kid's life bearable.

Thirty minutes later, Tyler was covered with sweat but smiling. "Thanks, Dad, I feel really good! I feel like I could touch the ceiling!" He jumped up high and got some sweaty house ape fingerprints on the door jamb.

I thought about pointing out the fingerprints, but then I realized something so obvious it hurt. I'd rather have a dirty house, shared with my two hopeless house apes, than a spotless house with no house apes at all.

That evening Tyler and I were sitting on the porch enjoying each other's company. I made fun of myself, somewhat apologetically, and how I lost my temper. Tyler laughed at the memory. Then he became very serious as he framed a reply to reassure his father.

"Don't worry, Dad – I sort of made an idiot of myself, too."

I've always recognized that a couple of house apes live in my house, just like when I was growing up. But on second thought, maybe it's three.

Take Care of Your Belongings

**Why did we waste money on a dresser
when your entire wardrobe is on the floor?**

Ann

Joseph had just returned from a couple of hours of "exploring" outside when I ducked into the laundry room to move a load of socks to the dryer.

"AAGHHH! Joseph, WHAT did you put in the sink?!"

Joseph excitedly popped his head around the doorway. It was a deer skull, of course! Wasn't it cool?

I steeled myself. "Um. Yes. It's very cool. What are you planning on doing with it?"

He planned to keep it – what else?

"I am so glad to hear that. Wonderful. I couldn't be happier. We can all look at it anytime we want." I paused. "And will you be keeping it in the sink?"

He looked at me somewhat uncertainly, and ventured that he was considering...his bedroom?

"Perfect. Let me get you a plastic container to put it in."

Thanks, Mom.

As the only female in a houseful of men, I

implemented basic survival strategies to preserve some household order, not to mention my sanity. One basic tactic was my rule that each of the boys put his belongings away. The kids claimed this antiquated practice was totally unnecessary – and highly annoying. Sometimes, Michael agreed.

Secretly, I questioned myself. What were my *real* motives for keeping a neat house? Was an organized home truly one of those important mom things? Or was it just a selfish, personal preference I was inflicting on my otherwise blissfully carefree men?

I envied Michael his ability to concentrate. He could sit in a living room chair with a laptop and work with single-minded concentration while the boys wreaked havoc around him. Michael claimed to value an orderly environment just as I did – but he had the mystifying ability to ignore the chaos when necessary.

For himself, I noticed he mostly adhered to his own rule, one that seemed to simplify his life immensely:

"Choose your battles wisely."

Mike

When Ann first became pregnant, I imagined fatherhood playing like a scene from the movie *Chitty Chitty Bang Bang*. In this tale, Jeremy and Jemima are bright-eyed, beautiful, tow-headed children belonging to Professor Caractacus Potts, played in the movie by Dick Van Dyke. These polite, attractive children sing delightful duets in perfect, smiling harmony throughout the entire movie.

With children like these, I'd be smiling and dancing the rest of my life, too.

But parenthood turned out different from what I had imagined. I never heard my kids singing happy duets, and I never got the flying car. Fatherhood was not the raising of beautiful, talented children who joyfully celebrated their childhood and seamlessly blossomed into the people God intended them to become.

Fatherhood turned out to be about survival - mine. And my children's.

I began to approach my responsibilities as a dad the way I would an operation. I paid attention to what was going on and endeavored to fix problems with a minimum of fuss and risk. Sometimes I did well; other times, not.

One afternoon, a new patient came to my practice for a second opinion. Surgery had been recommended to fix a large pelvic hernia. As a surgeon I agreed and wanted the chance to fix it. I knew two hours in the operating room would transform her anatomy from that of a tired forty-five-year-old mother to that belonging to a carefree twenty-five-year-old. But there was a signal problem - the patient's hernia was not bothering her.

With the exception of pain, or life-shortening cancer, surgery is best avoided when possible. Little benefit is realized from fixing anatomical problems that don't cause symptoms - and bad stuff can happen when your body is cut open.

So in this case, I advised against the operation. The patient was grateful. I had confirmed what she felt in her heart to be true. But just as I was patting myself on my back for good surgical judgment, I realized that, as a father, I'd been breaking my own rule about unnecessary surgery.

Tyler and Joseph were in the thick of their adolescent years. Coming upon Tyler's bedroom one Saturday morning, I had been appalled by its condition. His bed didn't have sheets, his dresser drawers were open, clothing and books were strewn over the floor.

It was a Disaster Zone. Or at least I thought so, until I stopped in to see Joseph, whose room made

Tyler's look spotless.

It's sometimes overwhelming to be a parent. Your job is to guide immature human beings into successful maturity until they can choose for themselves the path God dreamed for them. Occasionally, you are confronted with unmistakable evidence you are not doing your job.

What more proof do you need than a sloppy bedroom?

I experienced a moment of parental panic. Sloppy room, sloppy life, sloppy soul... *my boys were not on the path!*

In the ensuing weeks, I became the bedroom Gestapo, making surprise inspections morning and night, doling out strict punishment for any transgression. I was seized by a sense of responsibility for making sure my children knew how to keep an orderly physical environment. I felt that keeping their room clean was the key step to developing the discipline to succeed in life.

At first, Ann was pleased with my new regimen. By early adolescence, the boys had become expert at putting her off. She appreciated my active participation in daily discipline - and the kids' bedrooms were spotless.

But something began to nag at me. There was more discipline and organization in my home, but my boys were not smiling as much when I was around or sharing with me the details of their day.

It was as though we had assumed opposing sides in a battle.

I re-examined my surgical approach. The messy bedrooms that so bothered me were not actually causing my children physical pain. Kids have enough stress following the rules at school and negotiating their way through rapidly changing relationships with their peers... My bedroom inspections began to look like unskilled surgery. Isn't it more important for kids to feel safe and relaxed when they come home and have the chance to recharge their emotional batteries, than to have a clean bedroom?

So my technique for handling their slop once again changed. I maintained my "surprise inspections," but I eased up on the criticism and asked about their day instead. Lounging on a cushion in their room, I'd tell them about my day, too. We'd share some laughs. And whenever it was socially feasible, I'd end my inspection with a goodnight hug, telling them how important they were to me.

It was a more skillful operation.

And as far as their messy bedrooms were concerned, I just made sure to end with one key maneuver.

I shut the door.

Rules of the House

Um, just do what your mom says.

Ann

Michael and I began married life in a small apartment where we had no trouble arriving at a quick and simple agreement to divvy up the household responsibilities.

Michael would do the cooking, dusting, and vacuuming.

I would handle the laundry, the finances, and cleaning the bathrooms and kitchen.

Voila! This marriage thing was going to be a cakewalk. All those couples with marital disagreements - well, obviously Michael and I had a much more mature relationship.

The following night, Michael whipped up a spaghetti dinner with a package of cooked frozen peas on the side. I felt myself a fortunate bride with an attentive husband. I cleaned the bathroom that night to show Michael I would pull my own weight.

The next evening, there was no sign of Michael cooking. I rummaged in the refrigerator and found some leftovers. I didn't want to say anything and appear pushy so early in the marriage. The next night was the same. Finally, on the third night I ventured, "Um, Michael, I thought you agreed to do the cooking?"

He looked up and nodded. "Yeah."

"Well, it's been three days now since you made something."

He looked confused. "What?! You want me to cook every single DAY?"

As I came to know Michael better, I saw that he was willing to work hard – but at the same time, didn't mind dispensing with the rules every once in a while. On this account we are at opposite poles: I prefer order and routine. Once Tyler and Joseph were on the scene, this difference resulted in a significant gap in parenting styles. Decisions such as setting the boys' bedtime, for example, became something of a sore spot.

"Michael, the boys are not getting enough sleep. We have to be consistent about their bedtimes."

"I agree with you, one hundred per cent."

"Is eight thirty an acceptable time?"

"Perfect."

I was relieved to have a consensus. Or at least a fresh one. Michael was always hanging out with the kids at night, and getting them to bed was next to impossible.

That evening at eight-thirty, I called down to the basement for the boys.

"Okay guys – bedtime! Come upstairs and brush your teeth!"

No answer.

I called again.

Michael's voice floated up the stairs. "Annie – can you come down here for a second?"

I found the three of them gathered around the TV, laughing over one of those nature programs where a guy in camo is trying to catch an alligator. Michael looked up at me and wheedled, "C'mon, Annie – they can stay up just a half hour more. We're watching a really good show right now."

I was fuming. "Michael, we just agreed on a bedtime – TWO HOURS AGO!"

"I know, Annie," Michael said in a soothing tone. I stared in disbelief as he assumed an expression of patience. "You have to see the big picture here – family time is much more important than some arbitrary bedtime."

I went upstairs confused and annoyed. How did I always end up the bad cop? And why did Michael get to have all the fun?

I suppose one of Michael's strengths is keeping our focus on what he calls "the big rocks." Over the years, I have reconciled myself to his willingness to sometimes throw out the rulebook when he sees a better opportunity.

Conversely, Michael has learned to stick with at least a few rules – if only to make me happy. So on the occasion of our bedtime dispute, he agreed at least that the next time –

He'd back me up.

Mike

It was a Saturday morning, and Ann wanted the boys to finish their laundry. She swept into the family room where they lay sprawled on the couch in classic "I'm chilling out right now" positions.

"I need for you to wash your clothes and put them away by this evening," she ordered. "The machine has to be clear so I can do the sheets tomorrow."

The boys groaned and stirred sluggishly.

As the day wore on, the boy's sporadic and half-hearted efforts in the laundry room led to several more outbursts by Ann. The volume of her voice rose each time, and by the end of the afternoon, there were signs of a system overload.

"Joseph!" Ann said with one hand on her hip and

the other pointing at him, "YOU need to put your laundry in the dryer! The buzzer sounded two hours ago and if you..."

I had joined the boys in the family room and was reading. Joseph rolled his eyes resentfully at the start of Ann's diatribe. He put his book down and slowly rose off the couch but made no motion toward the laundry room. Instead, he stood in the center of the room and cupped his hands over his mouth...

"Nag Alert, Nag Alert. Incoming Nag! " Joseph intoned, mocking the computerized warning you might find on Air Force One if it were under a missile attack.

Tyler laughed and joined in the fun. "Deploy Countermeasures, Deploy Countermeasures!"

Joseph sauntered over to Ann and put his arm around her. "Mom, you look nice! Are those new earrings?" he said with an adolescent smirk on his face. His voice dropped to a monotone report. "Countermeasures Deployed, Countermeasures Deployed!"

Ann's smile had a strained quality. "I am serious, Joseph, you need to ..."

Joseph interrupted her. "I'm hit! I'm hit, I'm going down, I'm going down!" He circled the room, making crashing noises before throwing himself face down on the couch where he lay still, a faint smile on his face.

Tyler laughed, and so did I.

But a quick check of Ann's expression brought me to a halt: unlike the boys and me, she was not joining in the frivolity but instead looked upset. So I told the boys in no uncertain terms that their chores were not a joking matter. I added a glare for good measure.

But damage had been done already. Ann left the room in a huff.

Motherhood is like walking a tightrope. I'm pretty sure Ann didn't want to upset the boys by asking them to do their laundry. But she also knew they were out of clean clothes. Her desire for family peace gave her an unsolvable problem: put two teenage boys to work without diminishing the pleasure of their weekend. It was the Gordian Knot of Motherhood.

Fatherhood doesn't present the same sort of dilemmas. I don't really mind upsetting the boys. Sometimes I do it just for fun. And I have no idea about the status of their laundry, nor do I really care. It's their clothing, not mine.

Being a dad is a lot easier than being a mom.

I do, however, have a different kind of problem, a problem that is common to husbands: I care about my wife's happiness. My mentor Dr. Cross, with a wife, five kids, and umpteen grandchildren, once shared with me these words of wisdom:

"Happy Wife, Happy Life.
Unhappy Wife, Unhappy Life. "

So I ordered the boys to finish their laundry, *pronto* - or suffer the consequences of my wrath. They jumped off the couch.

I found Ann upstairs reading in our bedroom. She pretended she wasn't upset, but the pout was easy to spot. I asked her if she was okay.

"I don't think it's appropriate for you to laugh with the boys instead of backing me up."

Nag Alert, I thought to myself as I sat down next to her. *Deploy Countermeasures.* "I agree, Annie. You are one hundred percent right, and I told them so."

I paused. "By the way, sweetie, you look nice. Are those new earrings?"

She laughed.

We went out for pizza by ourselves. When we got back, the laundry had been completed.

Discipline
I'd rather play some video games.

Ann

When Michael and I started dating, he showed great interest in my artistic pursuits and in the fact that my sisters and I had spent hours of our childhood playing piano, painting pictures, singing, writing stories... At the time, I was highly flattered by Michael's attention.

In hindsight, I suspect he was just assessing my potential contributions to his gene pool.

After Tyler and Joseph were born, Michael allowed them a decent interval to get their bearings in the world and then began appraising their artistic skills.

"So, Annie, shouldn't you be teaching Joseph how to sing?"

I looked down at Joseph sitting in his high chair, a wide aimless grin on his face. Two and a half years old, he had shown zero interest in speaking - unlike his big brother, who had spoken early and often. Lately, I had come upon Michael in odd moments, holding his second son up to his face, staring at him, and muttering, "I'm just looking for signs of *any* intelligent life."

Joseph smiled wordlessly as he smeared oatmeal around the tray of his high chair. Despite my best efforts, I had been unable to encourage more than a few sounds from his lips. Singing a tune seemed out of the question. Seeing that Michael looked discouraged, I tried to say something hopeful. "It might be a little easier - you know, after he starts talking."

In my parents' house, for years the only spot for the piano was in the family room, twenty feet from Dad's TV. Stoically, he endured four daughters practicing piano after school, one after the other - often during the zenith hours of prime time TV. Dad heroically remained silent through it all, permitting himself only an occasional, long-suffering sigh.

As Tyler and Joseph moved through their grade school years, I couldn't see much resemblance between their interest in music and my sisters' and mine. I couldn't imagine forcing it on them. These kids could barely make it through their homework. By the time Tyler was twelve, Michael and I had resigned ourselves to the boys' utter lack of musical inclination. Then abruptly, Tyler developed a musical appreciation – for 80's rock guitar. I supposed it was a start, and Michael and I were pleased - at least until Tyler made his first musical request.

It was Christmas, and he wanted a video game called "Guitar Hero."

Now that there was a glimmer of hope for Tyler, my former apathy on the subject washed away in a tidal wave of anger, surprising me as much as anyone. Regardless of my share of responsibility, I directed my parental fury toward the Evil video game industry. Tyler watched in surprise as his mom threw a fit.

"I don't care if it IS Christmas!!!! We are not going to buy you some VIDEO game where you'll spend HOURS pretending to learn to play a guitar, when you could actually LEARN to play an instrument!"

With surprisingly little fuss, Tyler resigned himself to guitar lessons rather than "Guitar Hero," and Joseph followed a few years later on the piano, choosing it possibly for sheer size and volume. Thus Michael's dream of musical children finally came true.

My dad could have warned him.

Mike

When Joseph at age thirteen sat down to the piano after his first lesson, I experienced a moment of sublime joy. *My son, the piano player!* In my mind's eye, I saw Joseph receiving a standing ovation at Carnegie Hall, his voice cracking with emotion as he pronounced to the sold-out audience that he owed all his success to his dad.

But this reverie ended abruptly the moment Joseph's fingers pressed down on the keys.

When Ann and I were newlyweds, I admired her talents but reflexively flinched when she mentioned wanting a piano. Certain childhood memories of enforced lessons cast a black cloud over the whole subject for me. But Ann dragged me to an auction and persuaded me to spend $300 on a used upright, which sits in our living room to this day.

Ann is an accomplished pianist. In the evenings, while the boys and I lounge on the couch, she plays Bach or Beethoven. At Christmas, when friends gather round to sing carols, she accompanies for hours. But most of the time when Ann plays, I am in a different room, her songs wafting through our home, lifting me in ways of which I am barely conscious.

I regret not putting more effort into my musical skills. But I would never force my sons to take piano lessons as my Chinese mother did to Chris and me. I'd had no interest in learning to play the piano, and as the lessons ground on, there was only one thing I learned to hate more than practicing.

That was listening to Chris practice.

Chris must have learned more than one song in three years of lessons, but to this day, the only one I can recall is "Heart and Soul," the melody half of the old duet "Chopsticks." When it was Chris's turn to practice, no matter what our teacher had assigned, he would play this song over and over again. Thus I first became aware of the ungodly noises a piano can make.

Even so, when Joseph expressed interest in piano lessons, I couldn't help but feel hopeful. *Joseph will be a musician, like his mother, I thought...*

Joseph is a self-satisfied fellow. After his first lesson, he massacred a preschool piano ditty and immediately turned to me with his eyebrows raised smugly, like he had just played Beethoven's *Ninth*. This cocky attitude made proper parental encouragement a challenge.

"Oh, that was great, Joseph," I delivered my expected lines in a neutral tone. *Big whoop,* I couldn't help thinking. *Thirty bucks for **that?***

Over the next month, as Joseph practiced each day, I began once again to dread the sounds a piano can make. What Joseph lacked in skill, he made up in volume. I struggled to remain properly complimentary in the face of classic thirteen-year-old swagger. This was not easy. The kid expected applause every time he didn't fall off the stool.

Then something terrible happened: Joseph learned "Heart and Soul." And, just like his musically inept Uncle Chris, it was all he would play. After three days I lost it.

"Joseph!!! I can't take it anymore!" the words vomited from my mouth. "Are you *trying* to ruin my life?" I could feel my temple veins throbbing over the din. "Can't your stop practicing and watch TV instead?"

An unmistakable smile flitted across Joseph's face. Without pausing, he not only continued but played even louder. It appeared he would be quite happy to both practice the piano and annoy his father at the same time.

Ann was appalled. She motioned me to the other room. My job as a father was to provide encouragement, she emphasized with some agitation. How dare I jeopardize his fragile efforts in a new endeavor!

His fragile efforts? What about my fragile eardrums? But Ann was glaring at me. So I took a deep breath and bit my lip to keep more criticism from escaping.

God blesses us with children. Our job as parents is to guide them to become the best they can - hopefully without screwing them up too much.

But Joseph had been banging on those keys for over an hour. In my opinion, he needed encouragement less than I needed earplugs.

And then - a miracle!

"Oh my goodness, Joseph, what did you just do?!" I feigned eager astonishment. "It sounds simply fantastic!"

Joseph played straight man. "Yeah, Dad, I just stopped playing. I'm taking a break."

"Well, it sounds great!" I smiled proudly. "You definitely need to do more of that!"

I glanced over at Ann to see if this would pass as fatherly encouragement. She shook her head, face buried in a book, fighting back a smile. Ann would never admit it, but I suspect that she, too, was enjoying the peaceful sound of Joseph's fingers *not* pressing down on the piano keys.

Productive Behavior

Mom, XBox *is* productive. Look how many points I got.

Ann

There is one question I've always dreaded at the boys' annual check-ups:

Mrs. Litrel, do you limit your son's electronic entertainment to six or less hours per week?

I simply cannot answer the question directly. Mainly from sheer embarrassment. Yes, there have been weeks when the boys had more than six hours of electronics time.

Per day.

I've never understood what's so mesmerizing about video games. I dislike most TV programs. I don't like feeling that I am expected to fall into a trance-like state in front of the screen, being led like a mindless zombie from one commercial break to the next.

Even when Michael and I were newlyweds, I didn't want his television blaring through our small apartment, with our few leisure dollars going for cable service. Michael had a weak spot for the boob tube, but I also knew he felt guilty about watching in college and that he blamed at least one bad organic

197

chemistry grade on a good season of *Bonanza* reruns.

So I decided "no cable service" would be Michael's idea.

It was easy. A few conversations about weak-willed couch potatoes and how much time could be spent in prepping for the MCATS (med school entrance exams) instead of watching TV, and the better angel of Michael's nature soon rose to the occasion: he suggested we not subscribe to cable service.

I couldn't have agreed more.

For years afterward, Michael settled for one small TV and a set of rabbit ears, supplemented by a few Disney videos and a VCR player. However, by the time Tyler and Joseph were teenagers, those days were long past, and our basement had morphed into a "man cave" with three TVs, an Xbox, and two computers. Going down there set my teeth on edge, thinking how much more productively the boys could be spending their high school years.

Consequently, the boys' annual check-ups stirred up my dormant anti-TV angst. Michael would come home from work and ask innocently, "Hi babe, how was your day?"

"Great...um, I took Tyler in for his annual check-up."

The mood in the room would shift. Michael barely had time to brace himself before I was spilling out all my maternal anxiety.

"You know, Michael, all the research definitely shows the damaging effects of kids playing video games. The boys are just spending way too much time every day on their Xbox. I'd like us to consider disconnecting our cable service."

Michael sighed and arranged his face in a patient expression.

"Annie, isn't it enough that we keep ALL the television and electronics in the basement?"

Michael's next serious words were every bit a match for the pediatrician's. "Take a look at them. They're doing well in school. They're happy, they're not out doing drugs. They're actually socializing with their friends online. Do you know that?"

"Well, I guess if you put it that way..." I felt my righteous Mom backbone crumbling. I could never decide if Michael really had a better perspective on the boys than I did, or if he was just delusional. I clutched at the straw of hope he held out for me. Really, what did I know about boys?

"So, you really think that Tyler and Joseph are doing okay?"

"Absolutely."

Mike

I went into the basement after lunch one Saturday afternoon and found Joseph enthroned in his accustomed spot in front of the TV screen, playing a game called "Call of Duty" on his Xbox. I watched from behind him for a long moment as he expertly dispatched his virtual enemies with an assortment of alarming weaponry. A living room Rambo at age fourteen, he must have killed a thousand opponents in the hours he hadn't budged from his chair.

I took a deep breath and fought the overwhelming urge to throw his video-game-addicted butt on the floor and make him do pushups. In a pleasant tone of voice, I inquired how much longer he intended to play. For a moment, a worried expression clouded his face. But the shrug that followed conveyed exactly what he was thinking: *Father, why do you trouble me with such irrelevance?*

For this, I had no one to blame but myself.

No one argues for the benefits of violent video games; the debate is only about the extent of damage. Ann sides with the Academy of Pediatrics and remains vehemently opposed. I've learned from long experience that Annie is always right about these things.

And yet...

I remember the misery of being an adolescent boy: getting on the bus early mornings when it was dark, fighting through crowded hallways of grumpy kids, being trapped in a classroom with a boring teacher who droned on and on until the ringing of the bell signaled our return to the crowded hallways and yet another meaningless class.

During those tough years, my first stop upon returning home was my Atari game console.

My friends and I would huddle around the television set, venting our adolescent frustrations by endeavoring to outmaneuver the other guy and shoot down his digital blue biplane or blow up his red tank. Those were happy moments amidst unhappy early teenage years.

Video graphics have evolved in the past thirty years; they are a lot more realistic. But the satisfaction of blowing up your friend hasn't changed a bit.

Six years earlier, when Tyler had entered junior high school, the conversation shifted from Pokemon cards to Call of Duty. This best-selling video game arms you and a team of your friends with digital assault weapons for exciting combat missions against other teams. As Tyler pleaded for an Xbox, our parental "call of duty" was thrown into question. Do we forbid this and deal with the consequences of adolescent resentment? Or do we make our son happy by allowing violent games into our home and perhaps forever damage his soul?

I found myself arguing for the middle road. I made the case to Ann that our firstborn son playing Call of Duty alone in the basement wasn't quite as psychotic as it appeared. He and his friends were actually playing together online, strategizing, celebrating victories, bemoaning losses, and building friendships the clumsy way boys do.

At least he was venting adolescent hormones safely at home, instead of somewhere else with more opportunity for trouble.

Like many parents, we made a devil's bargain, linking Tyler's video time directly to his grades, homework, and chores: prove yourself responsible, pay for the box, and you can play.

By his senior year, Tyler hardly played Xbox anymore, and there were signs he was developing into a nice young man. I suppose this was reassuring, but watching my second son glued to the video screen as he killed all those realistic digital images troubled me just the same. Joseph was doing well in school, and he was keeping up with his responsibilities. But maybe we wouldn't be so lucky the second time.

I was biting my lip, lost in my thoughts as I stared at the back of Joseph's head. I didn't even hear Ann come up behind me. She asked me what was wrong.

Hearing his mother's voice, Joseph immediately put down his game control, got up, wrapped Annie in a gentle bear hug, and asked her how her day was going.

Ann smiled and answered, and after a moment, Joseph casually repositioned himself back in front of the television. Ann patted him on the shoulder and said she hoped he was having a fun day. Joseph politely assured her he was enjoying himself immensely and pointedly made eye contact. Ann left the basement with a smile on her face.

I thought about it some more and then stopped worrying. Joseph had made time for his mother. That was the promising sign I needed to see. I followed Ann upstairs - and left him alone.

Good Judgment

Hey Dad, at least I put the fire out.

Ann

Michael and I were both happy to see Tyler when he got back from two weeks at wilderness camp. It was the summer after his eighth-grade year. I hadn't been aware that I was worried about him until we saw him back at base camp unharmed. I felt an immense sense of relief wash over me as he rode beside us in the car ride home.

See, Ann? I said to myself. *There was nothing to worry about. Tyler was perfectly safe the whole time.*

"Well, I almost got killed," he said, as Michael went to grab his backpack.

"Really?" Michael seemed interested in a friendly sort of way. "What happened?"

"We were on a three-day kayak trip. It was a little rough, but it was getting kinda boring on the second day. Then we came to this place where we had to stop for lunch. The guide said we were going to come to a fork in the river, and he said we had to take the right fork, not the left, because it was too dangerous."

I tried to match Michael's casual tone. "So, what

did you do?"

"Oh, we took the left fork," he laughed, shaking his head ruefully, as though reminiscing about his childhood.

I froze inside. How was it that this perfectly intelligent child had deliberately disobeyed a direct instruction at a wilderness camp, of all places?

I knew what it was. When the boys were younger, I had refused to fill them with the accepted amount of fear and the usual nonstop precautions against walking alone in the woods or never climbing in high places. *Watch yourself in the road,* I told them, *you're the best one to keep yourself safe. Use common sense, stay out of dark places alone...* but I wanted my kids to know the pleasures I had known, wandering in the woods by myself, happily exploring, and NOT continually worrying about the sexual predators and freaks that fill the media spotlight nowadays.

Tyler went on with his story.

"Well, actually going down the wrong way was my idea. I had a kayaking partner. He was fourteen, but he mostly listened to me. I said, 'Hey Andrew, let's just give the left side a try!' Andy said, 'Tyler, the guide told us it was too dangerous!' And I said, 'Hey, what's the worst thing that could happen? We would just die a tragic and painful death!'" Tyler was laughing like a guy telling a good joke to his drinking buddies. "Andrew's eyes got all big, and he said, 'Umm... Tyler, that would be BAD.' But he went down with me anyway."

"Tyler!! Why did you do it!!?"

"I don't know - it seemed like a good idea at the time."

Mike

Just after my second son was born, I left Ann in the hands of her surgeon and followed Joseph to the nursery. Our newborn son was now the most vulnerable member of my family. I wanted to make sure he wasn't mixed up with someone else's baby.

But twelve years later, I wished he had been.

Arriving home from work, I found Joseph sulking on the couch. He wouldn't talk to me. I joined Ann in the kitchen to catch up on the day's events. Every few minutes, our conversation was disturbed by an intrusive sigh of woe.

I insisted Joseph tell me what was bothering him.

Joseph took a deep breath. "Do you remember that flint and magnesium you got me last year?" he opened rhetorically. "It's supposed to be for making fires. Well, yesterday I tried for an *hour* in the driveway, and I couldn't get a fire started." He looked up at me. "But today I finally did it."

A long pause.

"Well, that's good, Joseph," I said encouragingly, "isn't it?"

"No. Not really, Dad," he answered. "I, uh, lit the fire when I was sitting at the computer."

I try to keep my mouth shut when I get upset. Tight-lipped, I accompanied Joseph downstairs to survey the damage.

Growing more animated, Joseph explained how he had experimented, showering sparks on a piece of paper. This was apparently while surfing on the computer. A desktop blaze flared up. He swept the burning paper to the floor where the magnesium filaments set the carpet on fire.

He quickly stomped the flames out.

I took a breath. The damage wasn't terrible - just a CD-sized burn in the middle of the cream-colored carpet. Charred and melted, it was irreparable. But I swallowed my anger. *It's only stuff*, I philosophized, *and no one was hurt.*

Joseph's chagrined expression told me he wouldn't be setting any more fires for a while. But I took his flint away, just to be on the safe side.

Joseph continued to look upset. I couldn't blame

him. It hurts to do stupid things. I felt called upon to reassure him.

"Joseph, we all do things we regret. That's how we learn life's lessons." I was channeling Brady Bunch Dad, consoling one of his squeaky clean kids through a crisis. I had controlled my anger and communicated rationally. This was a proud parenting moment for me.

Joseph took a deep breath. "I'm not upset, Dad," he explained. "I'm angry!"

I knew exactly how he felt. "Sure, you're angry you did something dumb, right?"

"No - I'm angry at *you!*" Joseph declared. "I just think you should be thanking me more than you are. The whole house could have burned down - and I kept it from happening!"

My jaw dropped. "Excuse me!? Excuse me!!!??? You want me to THANK you?? Are you out of your MIND!!?" Now I was channeling Homer Simpson, my hands twitching with the desire to wring his neck. "You lit my carpet on fire, and now you want my *gratitude*!?!"

Joseph didn't back down. "This was a really stressful moment in my life, and I handled it well!"

"You set my carpet on fire!!!"

"I saved the house!"

This was one of those times when a twelve-year-old and a forty-four-year old were not going to see eye-to-eye. I suggested to Joseph that we separate ourselves from each other before the argument grew uglier. Defiantly raising his chin, Joseph huffed out of the room.

It was clear he couldn't agree more.

What a strange ride parenting can be, careening from joy to catastrophe and back again. I remembered my first glimpse of Joseph, a finger-sized fetus on ultrasound. It seemed that almost before I knew it, his tiny cries were filling the operating room, and we had borne witness to one of life's everyday miracles: microscopic cell to newborn baby in 280 days.

And twelve years later – proud pyromaniac.

It's an interesting phenomenon that those we most love are the same people who most annoy. It's normal family stuff, I suppose. We all have different needs and desires. For Joseph at twelve, it was playing on the computer and lighting fires and denying culpability. For me as a father, it was just keeping my sanity.

I could only pray that all future fires in our house – metaphorical or otherwise – were put out as quickly.

6

Faith

Ann

*There is so much
we need to teach the boys -
how to follow God
and to find His purpose for their lives.*

Mike

I think
we need to teach less
and learn more.

Recognizing God

God writes the best jokes.

Ann

Mom's father was a Presbyterian minister of boundless energy and faith. His influence extended into the third and fourth generation of his offspring. One of the many consequences of this was that my sisters and I grew up hearing Bible stories read to us by Mom over breakfast. Remembering this with a tinge of nostalgia, I resurrected the tradition for the boys' breakfast hour as soon as they were old enough to listen.

The boys' favorite story was David using a sling to kill Goliath.

"Do you think David aimed for the eye or the temple?" Tyler asked thoughtfully after one morning's reading. "Maybe the rock knocked Goliath's eye out!"

Gross. But I tried to match Tyler's thoughtfulness. "Hmmm... maybe." I wanted to say something to keep the lesson on track. "We're not sure about the details, but it's important to remember the point of the story: with God's help, even when we're small like David, we can conquer *anything*."

"But how BIG was the giant, Mommy?" Joseph wanted to know. He put down his spoon to gesture with his hands. "And how much BLOOD did he lose?"

"Umm... a lot." This was not turning out to be quite the moral lesson I had pictured. Apparently, God appeals to boys with stories different from those He uses with girls. I reflected that the Bible is like a variety pack: there's a flavor for everyone.

When I met Michael, he was a spiritually-minded agnostic. His religious roots were unusual: As a Chinese-Italian, he had Buddhism on one side and Catholicism on the other, and his whole family, loose and easy in the melting pot that is New York, was a bit free-wheeling when it came to established religion.

Within a year of meeting, Michael and I had formed a real attachment to each other. But for me, the relationship still faced a serious hurdle. As a Christian, I couldn't commit to a relationship with a non-Christian. Continuing to see Michael left me no choice: I was going to have to convert him.

His free-wheeling days were about to end.

I steered our letters and phone conversations toward sharing my beliefs about God and what it meant to be a Christian. Michael had a lot of questions. *What do you believe? How do you know God is a Person and not an impersonal universal spirit? What do you think happens to people who aren't Christians?*

I learned something from Michael, too: that God speaks to people who are outside established religions. Michael seemed to already have a distinct impression of God's presence in the world. I noticed the God who spoke to Michael was playful, a kind of cosmic Jokester who didn't mind spicing up His lessons with a few timely punch lines. Michael often related one particular story as an example of God's personal touch in teaching him humility.

Michael had always pictured his adult life as a prolonged season of carefree bachelorhood - dating younger women, driving a convertible, and sporting a full head of hair blowing behind him in the wind.

"Now look at me!ngaged to an 'older woman' when I'm only twenty-one. And *going bald.*" He shook his head, enjoying this private joke between him and God.

Mike

When I was growing up, Jenny was the family's gentle giant, an Irish wolfhound of 200 pounds. Her tail was a yard long and bony, wagging slowly back and forth like a metronome set on thirty beats a minute. Sometimes her tail hit the wall so hard it bled, spattering the wallpaper.

I recall one memorable evening when the sight of Jenny's happily wagging tail made me boil with adolescent resentment. What right had she to be so content when I was so miserable?

I was fourteen and listening to an angry lecture from my father. I'd broken my curfew. Again.

Ironically, for once I actually had a good excuse. A friend was heartbroken over his parents' divorce, and I had stayed out late because he needed someone to talk to. Helping in this way had been something new for me; I knew it was the right thing to do. So why was I about to be punished? It was a Cosmic Injustice.

My father's eyes were squinting as he stood before me in his t-shirt and underwear, conveying the nuanced shades of his anger. A crescendo in the lecture indicated he was approaching the finale, with the declaration of my punishment imminent. I dutifully nodded my head in time to his words, wearing a strategically ashamed expression on my face, in faint hopes of mitigating my sentence.

"YOU...ARE...GROUNDED!!" he roared, his finger pointed in my face. "You may stay in your room... UNTIL FURTHER NOTICE!"

Deflated, I trudged past him to my bedroom. Jenny followed me, her tail ponderously wagging. For some reason, I turned to ask my father what he meant by, "until further notice."

"It means... INDEFINITELY!" He warmed up for one last encore. "YOU ARE GROUNDED... FOREVER!"

As he jabbed his finger in the air, Jenny ambled past, her tail making a slow sweep through the air. My father was concluding his dramatic tirade with clenched teeth, and as he pounded a metaphorical gavel, sentencing me to life imprisonment, Jenny's tail completed its arc. At that exact moment, her rock hard tail cracked right into... my father's crotch.

"O-OWMPH!!" my father bellowed. He moaned and doubled over in pain, one hand holding his abdomen, the other on the wall to steady himself.

It was a Miracle.

I smothered an overwhelming desire to laugh and managed to ask my father if he was okay. Afraid I'd be unable to disguise the delight in my voice, I left him moaning there on the landing and hurried into my bedroom where I shut the door.

I giggled myself to sleep.

I woke the next morning, confused by a lingering sense of happiness. I remembered I'd been grounded, but for the life of me couldn't account for the smile that kept breaking over my face.

Then I remembered the Miracle of Jenny's Tail, and I began laughing all over again.

Maybe I was grounded, but that morning I recognized something important. A seed of thought began to germinate in the reassuring warmth that was permeating my heart -

Only God has such perfect timing.

Church Life

Mom, doesn't God love me even if I don't dress up?

Ann

Just before we got married, Michael became a Christian, and together we joined the local Methodist church where we planned to take our wedding vows. We agreed on the Big Picture: a daily prayer life, joining a church, and serving the community. After we started our family, the boys were easy to fit into the Sunday schedule, especially when they were small – drop them off at the nursery, and go on our way.

But as Tyler got older, he began complaining. Since Michael often ended up in the hospital working on weekends, I found myself again playing "bad cop," getting the boys dressed and off to church on Sunday mornings.

The spring the boys were three and six, I planned a weekend trip to visit my sister Jane. It was the first time I would be leaving my family for an extended time. I was worried Michael might skip the activities that were important for them, like reading bedtime stories, making sure they had fresh fruit with breakfast, and getting them to Sunday school. The changing routine might prove unsettling for the boys. I sat down with Tyler at the kitchen table to explain that I would be gone for a few days.

Tyler appeared to take the news well. He ran into the basement where Michael was watching television. Later Michael told me what he had said.

"Guess what, Daddy - Mommy's leaving town!! You know what that means!" he said excitedly. "THREE WHOLE DAYS with nobody telling us what to do!"

Mike

Many years ago, Ann and I we were late for a wedding, a large formal ceremony for one of Ann's college roommates. It was my fault. I had dawdled, confidently assuring Ann that weddings never start on time. Traffic slowed us further. Arriving at the Temple without a minute to spare, I found myself with an angry wife and no parking space in sight. I dropped her off at the entry and hustled for a parking space. The wedding procession was already underway when I finally made it inside.

There I was, the only guest standing outside the sanctuary. Thus I was sole witness to the bride and father in the moments before their entrance, the anxious daughter giving her daddy a piece of her mind. *Your bowtie is crooked, my dress is too tight, you're smiling too much...*

My timing was impeccable.

I snapped a few photos of the distracted bride and her father. Later the pictures proved a big hit - delighting Ann, a recovered bride, and most especially, her father.

Given this shared experience, I assumed Ann would not mind if the boys and I were late for her Christmas concert at church. The boys were eight and eleven at the time and didn't want to go. I couldn't blame them. I wasn't so keen on attending myself. I figured that the service would be candlelight with Ann singing up front. We could easily sneak in the back without her noticing and miss some of the more boring parts.

My timing could not have been worse. The sanctuary was lit bright as noon, the pews full to the bursting. Ann's fellow choir members were just lining up at the back of the sanctuary for their grand entrance. When the boys and I barged in late, all eyes turned our way. I scanned the sea of faces floating above the green choir robes and finally spotted Ann. Her expression conveyed extreme irritation. I was perplexed. Why such a dirty look? We were only a few minutes late.

I looked over at Tyler and Joseph standing beside me. They looked like they had come in straight off the playground. Joseph was wearing sweat pants, a tank top, and sneakers without socks. Tyler wore a stained white T-shirt which proudly boasted, "Pushing my luck is my only form of exercise."

Even by my less-exacting standards, I could see this was not appropriate Christmas concert attire.

In performing surgery, you sometimes find yourself in trouble. Suddenly the patient is bleeding, or the tumor is more extensive than had been estimated. Moments like these train you to gather your thoughts, evaluate the situation, and determine the best course of action.

I shoved Tyler and Joseph into the bathroom.

At least now we were out of eyesight from Ann and all those nosy choir members. I grabbed a wad of paper towels and swabbed at the dirt on Joseph's face.

I barked at Tyler to wash up. The water in the sink ran brown with mud. But I couldn't do anything about their wardrobe choices. I pondered a few moments before resigning myself to the inevitable: they would just have to change. We waited for the choir to file into the sanctuary and then we hustled back to the car.

On the ride home, I experienced a medley of emotions. I was resentful. We didn't even *want* to go to the stupid concert. I was worried. Ann had probably been humiliated in front of all her friends. I was angry. Are my kids morons who require I dress them and wash their faces? And I was self-recriminating. Am *I* such a moron I didn't even bother to look?

Despite attempts at self-restraint, angry words erupted from my mouth. *Don't you boys know what to wear to church? Are you both stupid? Are you trying to embarrass your mother?*

We pulled into the driveway and I stewed in the car as they changed their outfits. "You have three minutes," I said, "or you'll be grounded until *next* Christmas."

It was just enough time for them to get ready. But more importantly, it was enough time for me to cool down. This Christmas concert wardrobe fiasco was my fault, not my boys.' Children need guidance from their father, not unfair criticism.

So on the ride back to church, I apologized for yelling. Emotions are powerful, I explained, and sometimes we say and do the wrong thing. I asked their forgiveness. They readily agreed.

In retrospect, I suspect they just wanted me to

shut up.

At any rate, good spirits were restored by the time we reached the church. We couldn't help but notice the concert was now almost half over. And the boys were dressed so nicely in their turtlenecks and not-so-wrinkled slacks, I decided we shouldn't hide in back as originally planned, but should instead seat ourselves right up front, so Ann and the rest of her nosy choir couldn't miss us.

For the remainder of the concert, every time Ann and I made eye contact, I gave her my most charming smile. Maybe it was this, or the nice clothing, or simply the fact that Ann enjoys singing, but by the end of the concert she was no longer angry. "Michael," she said, laughing, "The boys look so *respectable*."

We drank punch and ate cookies afterward. Ann was happy, the boys were happy; it was another Christmas together. A feeling of contentment came over me, the same I experience after a difficult surgery.

It had been another successful operation.

Honesty

I thought you said you wanted the truth, Mom.

Ann

Michael and I hadn't heard from Tyler in a week. It was the summer of his eighth grade year, and he was returning from a mission trip in Appalachia, where the church youth group was building a new roof for someone's house.

I was eager to hear the details of this potentially life-changing experience.

"The house belonged to this old lady," Tyler explained. "She came out in the yard a couple times a day and she'd say, 'That roof there is lookin' real good...' " Tyler imitated her trembly country voice. "'I can't tell you boys what a load you're takin' off my mind.' "

He reflected a moment. "I gave up my whole spring break. But it was a good trade – I mean, a little old lady got a new roof."

My heart warmed. Finally, I thought, Tyler was growing up.

Unfortunately, he had more to share. "I really hated this one kid there. I think I almost killed him."

"Tyler!?"

"Oh Mom, he was a real jerk the whole trip. One morning he asked for a hammer. I was standing on the roof, so I threw it at him. He had to jump out of the way. He was really mad."

Tyler saw my horrified expression. "BUT," he added hastily, "there was this other kid, and I think I saved his life."

"Really?" I wondered if I sounded desperate.

"Sure, well... I think so. He was carrying a load of shingles up a ladder and started to fall backwards. I grabbed the front of his shirt and pulled him back onto the roof. It would have been a big fall." Tyler smiled. "He was REALLY grateful."

My emotions came to rest like a roller coaster car at the end of an amusement park ride. You want your children to be honest, but sometimes it can make you dizzy.

Mike

One winter morning I decided to save a few lives before catching the bus to junior high school. The water on the bird bath was frozen over. My mom had once explained to me that birds need fresh water in winter as much as they need food. So I grabbed the nearest heavy object from the kitchen counter, sauntered to the bird bath, and gave it a nice hard whack. Water welled up through the ice. I imagined throngs of thirsty birds watching from the nearby pine trees, filling the air with grateful chirps.

I was a hero. I was a fourteen-year-old boy a mother could be proud of.

But two days later, I found out I was neither.

"WHO CRACKED THE BOTTOM OF MY CRYSTAL WATER PITCHER?!!" my mother shrieked, brandishing a familiar heavy object. I hesitated just a moment before confessing. It was the only thing that saved me. Her next statement vaporized any inclination I'd had toward telling the truth.

"This is a WATERFORD LEAD CRYSTAL

WATER PITCHER!!" Mom's face was flushed, and her eyes bulged. "It cost OVER TWO HUNDRED DOLLARS!"

As though a dam had broken, my mind flooded with thoughts. *Lead crystal! No wonder it was so heavy! But how do you make crystal from lead? And who would pay two hundred dollars for a water pitcher? Man, I am so screwed, I am so screwed. I was just trying to save those stupid birds.*

Chris was bewildered. He gingerly touched the crack in the expensive pitcher. He was the picture of confused innocence. My mother glared at us, looking for clues.

I was dead in the water. Unless...

Quick as a flash, my face mirrored Chris's wide-eyed bewilderment. Then my lips pursed into a sympathetic pout... *poor Mom – her favorite water pitcher.* Then my eyebrows furrowed in a moment of deep concentration. Suddenly I realized who was to blame. I shot an angry glare at Chris. *How dare you hurt our mother! But brothers should not rat each other out. I know you did it, Chris, but I'll protect you this time!*

I resumed my expression of wide-eyed bewilderment.

Mom immediately saw through my brother's lies. Chris denied it, of course, swearing he had no idea what had happened. But Mom was too smart to fall for it.

I didn't believe him, either.

Thirty years later, when these less-than-proud moments came back to me, I was chagrined. I had just found the remains of my twenty-dollar Ace Hardware hose nozzle scattered across the driveway.

Still attached to the hose were the jagged remnants of my prized nozzle with its multiple settings.

What in the world had happened?! This could not have been done by a car. Nor was this the work of a wild animal or malicious prankster. No, this could only have been caused by an unthinking teenager.

Tyler confessed right away. The nozzle wasn't working right, so he tried to remove it from the hose. It was stuck. So he cut the nozzle off.

I looked at the jagged ring still clinging to the hose. What did you use to cut the nozzle off, Tyler? A lawnmower?!

No, that would be ridiculous. He had used an axe.

An ax? Did you consider a pair of pliers?

Tyler shook his head. He had tried that, and it hadn't worked.

I grabbed pliers from my toolbox. On my first attempt to twist the nozzle free, the top of the hose simply spun around. Tyler was pleased I was experiencing the same difficulty he had. But I grabbed a second pair of pliers to hold the hose tip steady, and the broken handle easily came off.

Tyler was dumbfounded: pliers obviously worked better than an axe. As we cleaned up the pieces, I commented that sharp metal objects left on the driveway can cause a flat tire. He was abashed. I was careful not to make him feel too wrong or too stupid. It had undoubtedly been faulty parenting. I must have neglected Father-Son Household Tools 101.

A teen is a clueless wonder. Strong and quick, he or she doesn't have the life experience to always act intelligently. For parents, letting go of broken possessions is the easy part of raising children. The hard part is preserving trust and communication. Sometimes understanding, and gentle correction, are all that's needed.

That - and keeping our prized possessions out of their reach.

Family Health Care
Reluctant doctor, doubting patients.

Ann

When Joseph was five years old, Michael took a fall and injured his arm. Joseph was fascinated by the appearance of the wound as it healed. One evening while Michael was reading, Joseph leaned in close for a look and then, picking up a pencil, began poking the injury to investigate.

"OW!" Michael said.

Joseph was startled. "Oh – sorry, Daddy."

"Joseph, you should be a doctor," Michael joked. "That way when you poke at someone and it hurts, you can at least charge twenty dollars."

Joseph apparently had no trouble believing this was the totality of his father's medical training. The next day while Michael was reading the paper after work, Joseph came over and again poked the wound with a pencil.

"OW!!!" Michael's brows came together. "Joseph, I TOLD you that hurt! What'd you do THAT for?!!"

Joseph coolly set down the pencil. He held out his hand and smiled pleasantly at his patient.

"That will be twenty dollars, please."

Mike

One weekend during my first semester of medical school, my father began quizzing me about eye surgery. It seemed he had just seen a TV show detailing the latest innovations in the field and wanted to direct follow-up questions to his someday-doctor son.

I confessed I didn't know anything. At the time,

my classmates and I were drowning in eighty hours a week of excruciatingly anatomy, physiology, and biochemistry. I remarked that we hadn't quite gotten around to eye surgery.

"Really...?" My father responded in an appraising tone. I knew what he was thinking: *Michael is not doing his schoolwork.* The shared memory of a certain upsetting parent-teacher conference loomed large and unspoken between us.

"Despite his potential, Michael is too immature to put forth appropriate effort. We must consider having him repeat the third grade."

I considered pointing out to my father that fourth grade had gone better.

The sad truth is, no matter what you do, members of your family will never take you seriously. Once, for example, I came home from work to find Ann miserably shivering on the couch under a layer of blankets. She had been sick for two weeks with a classic upper respiratory infection. Three days earlier, her headache had localized over her forehead. It was obvious sinusitis. I called in a prescription for an antibiotic.

Ann rejected the medication. "I'm not *sick,*" she clarified between sniffles. "I'm just... fighting something off."

I suggested the antibiotic would help her battle the infection.

"It's not an infection," she explained with indignation. "It's just a little inflammation."

Ann's reasoning was difficult for me to follow. According to the professors at my medical school, acute inflammatory processes are caused by infection.

Maybe Ann had learned different theories at University of Michigan's School of Art?

From the time I was young, I had craved the knowledge and skill to help others. Later, I worked my tail off to become a doctor. The emotions that energized me during this journey were love and compassion. But when I got home and found my wife on the couch with nary a prescribed antibiotic in sight, I didn't feel much love or compassion.

I was pissed. *I've treated hundreds of patients with upper respiratory infections*, I wanted to shout. *I didn't just look it up on the internet!*

A non-compliant patient is a challenge. Your recommendations are not followed, and your patient stays sick.

But it's even worse when that patient shares your bedroom. She remains ill and spreads her pox throughout your home. You may wish to discharge her from your practice, but marriage vows address this scenario with not just one, but two clauses: "for better or for worse" and "in sickness and in health."

You have taken a vow to love this non-compliant patient even though you want to send her packing.

Muttering, I drove to the pharmacy and picked up Ann's prescriptions. I helped her sit up, and in her weakened state, she accepted the medication I proffered. I stood over her as she swallowed it. Exhausted, she collapsed her head back on the pillow.

I went to the kitchen sink and turned on the faucet. After the water warmed, I lathered my hands and fingers for thirty seconds to wash away any clinging germs from my wife's body.

"Thanks for getting me my medicine," Ann

called weakly from the couch.

I told you so, was what I was thinking. "I hope you feel better," was what I said. I didn't feel the love and compassion in my voice, but at least I got the words right.

Then I retired to a less germ-infested room.

Setting Wrongs To Right

**The only thing I'm sorry about
is you insisting I apologize.**

Ann

One Halloween, I got a call in the middle of the school day from Joseph's Spanish teacher. It wasn't good news.

It was difficult to modulate my attack on Joseph as he came through the door that afternoon.

"Joseph! Your Spanish teacher called and said you were being racist! She said you dressed up as an Hispanic immigrant for Halloween?!! And then you made fun of your classmate's Spanish accent!!?"

A look of utter confusion came over Joseph's face. *This kid needs to be up for an Oscar,* I thought.

I repeated his teacher's charge: Joseph Litrel had come to school dressed as a person of Hispanic descent for Halloween and then made fun of people with Hispanic accents. One offended classmate reported the incident to his father, who then called the teacher.

Joseph's outrage was instantaneous. "I DIDN'T dress up as a Mexican for Halloween!! There was a sombrero on the shelf in Spanish class, and I picked it up and put it on. And then I said, 'Look!! Soy Mexicano!' Then everybody laughed, and we just ate the tacos and party food!"

"Really?" That didn't sound so bad.

I felt a sense of relief. But some action seemed required. "Joseph, I think you'll still need to straighten this out. Apologize to your classmate, or at least explain. He misunderstood, and you hurt his feelings."

"NO!! I refuse! This is stupid!! He is TOTALLY making this into a big deal!"

I struggled for some words of wisdom. "Sweetie, you and God will always know the truth. And I believe you. BUT what that boy THOUGHT you meant is the point here, and I'm going to ask you to call him to explain and say you're sorry." I paused. "That's BEFORE you get on your computer this afternoon."

"Fine." Joseph seemed suddenly ready to shelve the protests.

I watched as he found the phone number with great efficiency, made the call, and matter-of-factly apologized to his classmate. Then he asked to speak with the father. "I truly didn't mean to say anything offensive, sir, and I am really sorry if anything I said came across wrong. I did not mean to offend anyone."

It was over so quickly. Joseph turned to go back downstairs where his afternoon computer game was waiting. He was quite chipper.

Mike

By the time Tyler reached his senior year of high school, he had outgrown some of his earlier unhappiness. He explained adolescence this way:

"When I was thirteen, I hated everyone and everything, and everyone and everything hated *me*."

I remember those years when Tyler and I found

each other mutually annoying. Sometimes Tyler sighed, occasionally he screamed. And sometimes he grumbled half-humorously, *Hulk get angry. Hulk not want to listen. Hulk want to SMASH...*

My expectations were that Tyler perform well in school and take on some household responsibilities. These expectations were diametrically opposed to Tyler's - namely, that he do whatever he wanted, whenever he wanted.

No one wants to be told what to do all the time, particularly an adolescent, so I usually allowed some leeway. Three hours on the computer before bed seemed excessive to me, but why not let Tyler finish his stupid game? So what if he was sprawled on his bed in a pile of dirty clothes and candy wrappers? Why not shut his bedroom door instead of screaming like a banshee? My goal was to guide my children, not control every aspect of their lives.

But my tolerance had its limits.

One day during Tyler's seventh grade year, Ann received a call from his English teacher. Tyler had run out of class just before the last bell at the end of the day. Although Miss Andrews called out for him to return, Tyler just laughed - and left. Ann was mortified. When I got home that day, she relayed the news and asked how I thought we should proceed.

I found Tyler lounging in his bedroom. I mentioned that his teacher had called. I asked him what had happened. He laughed as he told me the story - and he had his excuses lined up. *He wanted to get home to see me. He wasn't laughing at Miss Andrews, he was laughing with her. His friends dared him, and he wanted to prove he could do it...blah, blah, blah...*

I decided this was a time for focused action with minimal fuss. I made the first incision.

Tyler, you are grounded. No TV, no computer, no electronics. You cannot leave your bedroom except for meals or the bathroom.

Tyler was shocked. "That's unfair! I didn't do anything! I was just kidding around! Miss Andrews is being crazy! It was no big deal!"

And you must write an apology letter to Miss Andrews.

Tyler fell on his bed and began kicking and punching his mattress. He screamed into his pillow and twisted around in his sheets.

As I watched Tyler's spectacular tantrum, I pondered the question of how long his punishment should be. It had been a nice day, until this news about Tyler arrived. Now instead of relaxing, I had to teach an immature human being with under-developed social skills how to behave in a responsible and respectful manner. I was embarrassed by my son's lack of manners – and worried. Maybe Tyler was destined to be a delinquent? Why didn't I ever get calls about how *well* my son had behaved?

Inspiration struck.

Tyler, you are grounded until Miss Andrews personally calls me on my cell phone. She must tell me that not only has she has accepted your apology but also that you are an excellent student whom she is delighted to have in her class.

Tyler began to cry. "Dad, please, please, Dad – not that, not that! How am I going to get her to do that?"

I have absolutely no idea. That's your problem, not

mine.

I closed his bedroom door and went downstairs. Ten minutes later Ann and I could still hear muffled screams from his bedroom and the unmistakable sound of his head hitting the wall.

I had doubts how this operation would turn out. I decided I'd ground him two weeks before changing the parameters I had outlined. But the very next afternoon, as I was seeing patients, my cell phone rang. A hesitant voice was on the line. I had been expecting a nurse from the hospital, so it took me a few moments to place the caller. It was Miss Andrews.

"I just wanted you to know that Tyler was very well behaved today. He wrote me a really nice apology note. You know... he is almost always a good student. I'm very happy to have him in my class."

I thanked Miss Andrews for her dedication and commiserated with her about how difficult young teens can be. I invited her to call me or Ann anytime we could help. I found myself smiling when I got off the phone.

What a pleasant experience it had been to receive good news about my son. But I had to admit, the experience left me with a bit of a mystery.

How the heck did that immature kid get his teacher to call me?

In Sickness and In Health

Get your germs away from me.

Ann

When I was forty-one, I had another bleed in my brain.

I was working on a collection of paintings for my next art show. Wildly colored images filled my imagination, with shapes and lines of unearthly beauty. But I couldn't get them to come to life on the canvas. For six months I struggled. I wasn't sleeping. I was getting a strange metallic taste in my mouth. Michael told me point blank I had to slow down, or I was going to make myself sick.

Five weeks before the show, I had the bleed. It put me in the hospital for another two weeks. I was so weak when I finally came home that the bedcovers felt like a lead blanket. I was unable to do anything, for anyone – including myself. I wasn't a wife. I wasn't a mother. I wasn't an artist.

I was a patient.

Neighbors and friends stepped into our lives to take care of me and the boys. Each day brought a different friend taking a turn at my bedside, watching over me while Michael was at work. Night after night, a full dinner was delivered to our house by first one neighbor, then another. Even our sweet mail lady made us a homemade pie.

God was clearly at work in the world.

Then one morning after a month had passed, I found myself lying in my bedroom alone. I felt the familiar cloud of almost overwhelming tiredness and fear. Suddenly, it seemed urgent that I start moving again. It was almost a Voice, saying, *Now or never. If you are going to live, if you are going to take care of your family again and stop being a patient, it is time to get up.*

NOW.

I struggled up and made my bed. I asked Michael to let everyone know we wouldn't need dinners delivered to the house anymore.

Of course, Michael was happy I was feeling better, but he seemed a little disappointed about the dinners. He ventured it had been nice to have the doorbell ringing every evening, to see a smiling face holding out an armful of home-cooked goodness. He went so far as to suggest that he bring a wheelchair home from work and take me out for one more turn around the neighborhood, so everyone could see. Maybe we could score a couple more weeks of free meals?

I presumed he was joking, but with Michael, it's sometimes hard to tell.

"Just think about it, Annie," he said. "We could probably milk this meal thing for the rest of the year!"

Mike

The occasion of my first health scare came right after the Christmas that I'd finally purchased a big screen TV for our basement. The two events were connected.

For years, the one-hundred-eighty-dollar set I'd bought at Kroger had worked just fine. I didn't mind that a grocery store TV was a source of embarrassment for my children. Side benefit: at least they weren't spoiled with expensive electronics. I also didn't mind that my friends preferred their house to mine at Super Bowl time. Side benefit: we'll watch at your place - and what are you cooking, anyway?

But I drew the line when a smoke smell started coming out of the back.

With a mixture of anticipation and dread, I ventured into Circuit City and chose a new home theater system, under the guidance and encouragement of Tyler, then ten years old. Two days before Christmas our selections arrived in several obscenely big boxes, along with an installation crew.

This should have sounded a warning bell. My Kroger TV set had simply slipped out of its box like a TV dinner, ready to plug in and serve. It was not big, nor was the picture good, but it had certain qualities I had never appreciated until my theater system was set up.

For starters, I could actually turn it on. There was a power button and a couple of controls for channels and volume. With these simple functions and a remote control, I was the unchallenged king of prime time TV.

Not so with my home theater system. Suddenly I was introduced to a whole new vocabulary – input, video, antenna, PIP - strange elements that required perfect alignment to allow me to watch my show. An instruction manual existed, but it was as dense as my college calculus textbook and destined for the same fate – being flung on the floor in a moment of frustration.

I'd plant myself in front of the television, point the remote at the rebellious screen, and grow more and more agitated as it refused to submit to a channel change. So for the first month or two, I did what many do when it comes to new technology: consult the expert of the house. In this case, Tyler. Impatiently, he would roll his eyes in shades of preadolescent exasperation as he adjusted the television to accommodate his father's wishes.

Finally, I called the installer and made an appointment for him to show me, once and for all, how to work my TV. I left plenty of time in my schedule. With eagerness I anticipated mastering the fine art of home theater operation from someone who could properly explain the concepts.

An hour before my appointment, I got a call from the hospital. A colleague needed assistance with a difficult surgery already underway. I called Ann as I raced up the road. I told her about my all-important appointment with the TV installation technician.

Ann pointed out she had no interest in learning how to work the home theater system. It's my TV, she doesn't watch TV, and she was overbooked today. Why should she change her plans to meet with a TV guy?

My chest began to hurt just talking about it. I was more annoyed than worried. But I saw an opportunity.

"This conversation is giving me chest pain," I declared. "I need you to do this, and I need to get off the phone."

Well, now Ann was worried. She capitulated and kept my appointment with the technician, taking two pages of notes. I came home that evening and learned to work the system like a pro – surround sound and everything.

But the chest pain lingered and intensified over the next ten days whenever I felt stress. Work, marriage, children, all the things usually so joyful now seemed physically unpleasant. Truthfully, I was worried about my health. But like many men, I did what comes naturally. I ignored it. We were due to leave for a vacation in Mexico, and I was busy. The last thing I needed on my schedule was a doctor's appointment.

Or so I thought. The morning before our vacation, Ann muttered something about somebody getting chest pain every time things didn't go his way and somebody keeling over on vacation in a third world country. When I arrived at the office, my nurse Danielle told me that all my patients had been cancelled. I was dumbfounded. She directed me to the cardiologist.

Ann had made an emergency appointment.

A little complaining is a dangerous thing. I resented having my morning stolen from me. There were many patients who had waited to see me, and now here I was, wasting valuable time *being* a patient. An attractive nurse shaved the hair on my chest to place the EKG leads for the stress test. Miffed, I made a mental note to mention to Ann how pretty she was.

I ran a dozen minutes on the treadmill. My stress

test was negative. The chest pain was probably coming from my stomach. The doctor wrote a prescription to give to Ann. "Heart is fine – may go to Mexico."

Later, Ann and I laughed about my shaved chest as we lounged by the hotel pool, and even though I tried several times to make her jealous about the pretty nurse, I no longer felt resentment. I felt gratitude. Life would be lonely without the people who love you, lecturing you, worrying about you, and sometimes forcing you to get the help you need.

Even if they give you chest pain.

Learning Compassion

I used to look up to you, Dad, but now you're throwing like a girl.

Ann

Beginning when they were five years old, Tyler and Joseph each spent their summer days outdoors in a local old-fashioned camp. When Joseph reached high school age, he and his fellow campers were sometimes loaded into vans to volunteer in downtown Atlanta.

One day he came home in an indignant huff. He had spent the day in downtown Atlanta's "Shantytown," where cardboard boxes line the embankments under the downtown overpass, serving as shelter for some of Atlanta's homeless. I remembered that twenty years before, Michael had done his medical training not a quarter mile away at Grady Hospital. Apparently, not much had changed.

Joseph explained that he and his fellow counselors had been given a cooler of food, with instructions to hand each person they encountered a sandwich, an apple, and a drink.

"And guess what!! I got in trouble!! We came up

to this REALLY big guy, maybe three hundred pounds. I mean he was WAY over six feet. One measly little sandwich just didn't seem right -

"And then the head counselor started yelling at me! 'Joseph,'" he mimicked, "'Just one sandwich apiece. No more.' I don't get it!" he fumed. "We never even used up the rest of the sandwiches! So what were we saving them for? Just some stupid rule!!?"

He looked around at his childhood home, warm and well-stocked. "Mom, they were just living in cardboard boxes."

Mike

When Tyler was in elementary school, watching me throw a football often made his jaw drop in awe of his father's physical prowess. It was beyond his imagination that another human being could be so strong, so athletic... so manly. Those were fun parenting moments - the "Wow, Dad, you're amazing" years.

Times change. As a teenager, Tyler still dropped his jaw when I threw the football deep. In disgust, not admiration.

"Your passing s&#*ks, Dad!" Tyler shouted as he trudged empty-handed back from the end zone. Joseph, Tyler, and I were losing to Tyler's friends. Tyler muttered to himself as he walked back to the huddle. I couldn't quite hear what he was saying, but I knew it was pejorative language directed at me.

I felt defensive. *It was a good throw, Tyler! You just didn't run hard enough!*

Good THROW?!! Tyler spread his arms in disbelief. *It was in the STREET!!*

NO, it bounced out of bounds when you let my pass SAIL between your hands!

Are you out of your MIND?! Tyler's eyebrows rose incredulously.

Tyler's friends, Alex, Walter, and Mitchell, wore

big smiles as they listened to us argue. Tyler was right; it had *not* been a good throw. We'd had a chance to make the play, *if* Tyler had run like a rabbit and leaped like a gazelle. Instead of a middle-aged athletic blunder, it could have been a glorious touchdown pass.

When the boys were little, I was the uncontested star. But by the time the boys had reached their teens, I had become the annoying big guy who thinks he's good but sucks.

"You quarterback, Tyler," I said confidently. "I'll show you how to catch the ball."

I hiked the ball to Tyler and hustled to the end zone as fast as I could. I saw the ball coming over my left shoulder; my eyes were glued to it like a laser beam. I wanted nothing more in my life than to make that touchdown. But just as the ball passed over my head, a clump of green flashed in the corner of my eye. It was the magnolia tree. With my arms raised upward, I careened into the trunk. Branches clawed my body, and one limb gouged me in the chest. The ball hit a branch just over my hand and bounced off to the side.

Not only was it an incomplete pass, but I was also in considerable pain.

The boys laughed happily. As I extricated myself from the tree, tears welled in my eyes. Thank God for sunglasses.

"You really should have held on to that one, Mr. Mike," Alex said with a laugh.

Back in the huddle, Tyler was still chuckling. "Boy, Dad, that pass went right through your hands. Next time you gotta try harder."

His laughter made me angry. "You know, Tyler," I responded, "it's more fun watching somebody smash into a tree than actually doing it."

Tyler's smile vanished. "I'm sorry, Dad. It was a really bad pass." He slapped me on the shoulder apologetically. "But you made a really good try for it, a really good try."

I felt strangely mollified. My adolescent son had acknowledged I'd done my best – instead of laughing about what a loser I was. The next play, I threw a better spiral, and Tyler dug deep to make the score.

We played another half hour. Ann brought out a tray of cold drinks. We sat on the driveway and argued about the final score, who had made the best plays, and who the worst. No one really cared. We were dirty and sweaty and tired.

It was a perfect game of touch football.

Love
**We are given everything we need –
except the sense to realize it.**

Ann

One day Joseph came home from middle school extremely upset. His teacher was losing her job and had spilled out her troubles to his class. "She has a baby, and she said her husband is out of work. Mom, it's really bad!"

It did sound hard. But I was a bit indignant that a teacher was unloading her personal problems on students, unformed teens who were ostensibly her responsibility. These kids were powerless to help. They could only go home with bad feelings or undeserved guilt.

I was mad at Joseph's teacher on his behalf, and I let him know it.

Joseph's response took me by surprise. He was angry at *me*!

"Mom! You're totally wrong!! It's not bad that she told us! You weren't even there. What if we can help her? What if we can make her feel better?!"

He related how he and his classmates had banded together and written cards to the teacher and even pitched in for a gift. Then at last he showed me the personal thank you note she had written to him later, telling him that his note had meant the world to her.

I was humbled. Playing the protective parent, I had missed the most important point. My child was not a helpless being, floating through the world like an aimless victim. He had the power to act, to communicate, to show compassion for others – and to make a difference in the life of another person, one whom I had never met.

I recognized God, sharing His wisdom through my child.

Mike

A mission trip to Honduras with Tyler seemed an inspired idea. I was seized with a vision of my teenage son forsaking his Xbox for a transformative week of caring for poor people in a third world country. We boarded a flight with twenty others from our church, headed on a small plane for the capital airport, and then rode a bus to the rural mountain area.

Our physical task was to repair homes. Our spiritual task was to learn and teach about God's love.

Tyler was shocked by the poverty we encountered. Forty people lived in the remote village, in huts made of mud and sticks. They had no running water or electricity. There was a brick school building that members of our church had helped build a few years before. There was also a single cinder block outhouse. The dogs that wandered the village were so emaciated you could count each rib.

Over the days that followed, Tyler took me to the side several times to sort through his feelings. How could we have so much at home - gifts from God - when others in the world have so little?

I was proud of Tyler. He was growing up, asking the right questions - but as it turned out, he was still an obtuse adolescent. On the last day, we faced a three-mile hike to the most distant work site. Steep hills made the steaming Central American jungle even more challenging. As we set out, Tyler assured me he had filled all our water bottles. But when we arrived, I discovered only three of the eight bottles were full. Tyler had gotten lazy and just hadn't bothered.

I was livid. We had an entire afternoon of physical labor ahead of us. The water from the stream would only make us sick. I sputtered a parental diatribe at Tyler. But since we were on a Christian mission trip, I toned down my expletives.

Don't you realize we have four THOUSAND pounds of cement to mix? How can we work without water? Blah, blah, blah...

I'm sorry, DAD!!! I GET it! Tyler threw up his hands in exacerbation.

I could tell that Tyler was more angry than sorry. But I stopped my lecture and sulked away, muttering dark thoughts under my breath. I had been proud that Tyler had chosen to come along. Of the twenty in the group, Tyler was the youngest by five years. Heaven knows it was gratifying to see his hands finally off the game controller and wielding a shovel full of dirt.

But I didn't want to hear any adolescent fibs about filling water bottles just before our hike into a jungle.

Our worksite was a hut, with a dirt floor we were to replace with one of cement. Twenty bags of mix had already been carried to the site. The choice of tasks were these: carry buckets of water from the stream, mix the cement on the ground, carry the wet cement into the hut, or lay down the floor. There were eight of us. It was back-breaking work.

Three hours later, we lay exhausted under the hot equatorial sun. We surveyed our halting progress. A feeling of discouragement began to creep over the group. The floor was only a third done, and we were running out of both cement and energy.

I slumped on a stool, under a tree that sheltered a dozen tamed parrots. Within a few minutes, a six-year-old village girl named Amalia came over and quietly sat next to me. Her dress was worn, her face was dirty, but her smile was beautiful. She was one of the eight children who lived in this tiny hut with the dirt floor. A cement floor would keep her young body off the ground at night.

Tyler was resting motionless nearby, his back against a tree. His work efforts that afternoon had been listless at best. I felt he should have been working harder, but I kept my criticism to myself. At least he was here with me.

Just when finishing the job seemed hopeless, several natives from a neighboring village appeared in the distance, walking along the path to our worksite. They had come to help. Recharged, we resumed mixing cement, carrying bucket after bucket into the hut. Somehow, we now had so much that we could not only cover the entire dirt floor but even make a front porch.

Remarkably, too, our water bottles never ran out. Tyler and I had enough to last the entire afternoon.

It was a strange and wonderful day in Honduras. Tyler and I had partaken in a kind of miracle: plenty of cement, a floor for Amalia, and even enough water.

For me, it was a spiritual reminder that we are always given enough - an ironic lesson to learn while helping a family whose belongings could fit in the trunk of my car.

It was only later, as I was falling asleep, than I figured out –

Tyler had left all the water for me.

Epilogue

She Said, He Said

Ann

Michael, isn't it amazing to think we've been married twenty-five years?

Mike

I know.
This is starting to get serious.

Looking Back On 25 Years

Marriage is a life sentence.
And sometimes it feels that way.

Ann

It was summertime. Michael and I were making plans for our 25th anniversary, fast approaching in October. I pictured a party and a dance floor jam-packed with three or four hundred people – everyone who had been a part of our lives through the years. The evening would culminate with a beautiful renewal of our vows, with Michael and me standing side by side wearing black and white, just as we had on the night we met and then on our wedding day, twenty-five years ago.

Michael agreed it was an interesting idea. However, he wasn't crazy about the party. Or the dancing. Or all the guests.

Or even renewing our vows.

"Why would I want to do that?" Michael looked irritated. "I meant my vows the *first* time around."

A few months previously, Michael and I had discussed the idea of putting together a book about marriage and family, based on stories he had published over the past decade. Michael suggested that this book – a "he said, she said" rendition - might be a good way for us to celebrate our anniversary. What could be more fitting than a testimonial on what we had learned from our marriage and raising the boys?

I agreed.

Through the long summer days, I wrote. Joseph left each morning to volunteer at camp. Tyler was making preparations to leave for college, having just graduated from high school. Each morning he chatted with me in a friendly way and then hopped into his car to make the rounds with his friends every afternoon before they too left. He packed up his room; I saw his carpeting for the first time in years. Michael was at work, and I was alone. My hours at the computer were punctuated with bursts of sobbing that seemed to come over me all on their own. I tried to suppress them quickly so I could concentrate on my work.

The summer was beginning to feel like a bookend on my life as a mother. What had I learned from all this? Had I been a good wife to Michael, a good mother to my boys?

As I wrote about Tyler sleeping through his homeschooling, I wondered why I couldn't have made him more academically curious. As I wrote about Joseph playing video games, I questioned how I could have made him persist in scouting instead of racking up Call of Duty points. And as I catalogued the boys' endless feuding, I wondered what moments I had missed in showing them how to love each other better.

Then one morning, as I was writing, I had a vision of myself, as though God were allowing me to see Ann through His eyes. And what I saw was a worried wife and mother, measuring her family against some invisible standard, a mythical perfect family she imagined must exist somewhere.

I felt a flood of regret. In trying to be the perfect wife and mother, how many fun, messy moments had I missed, striving to shove Michael and my boys into some rigid cookie cutter pattern for a family that wasn't even real?

For instance, I had wanted regular sit-down meals, no TV. I saw that Michael had balanced my impulses with miraculous, spontaneous family moments - a marshmallow fight or a pig-out at the donut shop.

I had always resented feeling like the "bad guy." Now I saw it wouldn't have been the end of the world if I'd eased up a little bit. The boys appeared to have survived not always eating their vegetables, and playing hours of video games.

Struggling under the weight of my questions and doubts, I found the writing slow. Our publication deadline was looming. Michael's schedule was tight. Every morning before he went to work, we went over my progress on the draft. As the stress increased, we argued. A lot.

Our little husband-wife book project was not the romantic anniversary activity we had envisioned.

The fighting reached new heights. After one particularly bad morning, I hunted down a quote I recalled from former President Jimmy Carter, who described co-authoring a book with his wife Rosalynn as, "the worst problem we've ever had since we've been married."

I took some comfort in seeing that their marriage had survived, but even so, I could see that writing a book about marriage… was ruining our marriage.

We cancelled the book launch.

And we took a vacation. Just the two of us on an anniversary trip. No kids. And definitely no laptops.

Michael and I went to Sedona, Arizona, a famous artist's haven surrounded by spectacular red cliffs and blue, arching skies. On the first morning we arrived, we set out to visit one of the region's famous energy vortices, supposedly conducive to energy and healing. As we climbed into the morning sun, we passed a woman sitting on a rock, who intoned, like a self-assigned tour guide, that we were visiting the Vortex of Balancing Male and Female Energy. Male energy is anger, she added helpfully. Female energy is fear.

Great. We figured a little balancing wouldn't hurt.

We climbed to the top and sat on the red boulders and rested in the sunlight. We held hands and laughed, and the months of arguing fell away in the sun like an unneeded coat.

In the evening, Michael drove me to a beautiful spot, a rocky stream at the foot of Cathedral Rock and a vantage well known to artists and photographers. As the sun began to set, a thin crescent moon rose in the sunset sky, electrifying the visiting artists and photographers swarming everywhere. I was swept up in the energy, sketching and snapping photos every minute as the unearthly light glowed and changed everything it touched. Everyone vibrated with the energy of this heavenly scene. Only one visitor seemed unengaged – Michael.

He lay on the rock in the setting sun. He had pulled his cowboy hat over his eyes, taking the opportunity for a quick nap while his wife satisfied her artistic whims. Artists and photographers swirled around him like snowflakes in a blizzard, sketching frantically or snapping photos, as he lay still like the eye of a storm, peacefully sleeping.

I looked at him in wonder. *Was Michael enlightened? Or just oblivious? What did he and I have in common, anyway? And what on earth would we do together for the next twenty-five years?*

At that moment the marriage really did seem like a MisMatch. It was a relationship between a man and a woman, an artist and a surgeon, a rule follower and a rule breaker. Our family life was always in turmoil - our sons had fought constantly. In fact, the whole dang family was one Big MisMatch.

But as the light shifted, I suddenly saw Michael's face, still like the center of a storm – perfectly peaceful, immovable.

All the thoughts that had been swirling in my head for the past few months came together. I saw that perhaps too often I had lived my life focused on what was missing in my family, instead of what I had – on what I imagined family life would be – instead of what I had been given.

Like a quiet voice, I heard the thought: *Perfection is not to be found on this earth.*

Yes, my family was a MisMatch - like most families, I imagined.

But in this one clear moment, I finally saw that God had given me exactly what I had needed for me to learn in my life. He had indeed made this MisMatch.

Just for me.

Mike

Recalling our adventures raising a family has brought home to me the many life lessons that a man - and a physician - can only learn from a woman.

When I entered medical school, Obstetrics and Gynecology was the specialty at the very bottom of my list. And that included Proctology.

My impression of Gynecology was based wholly on a former girlfriend's reaction to her first GYN exam. When I asked how it went, she just shook her head and grimaced. I thought I could even see a few tears in her eyes. I knew then that GYN was one field I would make it a point to avoid like a minefield.

God has a sense of humor.

Years later, as a third-year medical student, I entered the hospital for the first time to learn how to take care of patients. I was assigned to Labor and Delivery, under the supervision of a firm-minded intern in her first year of training in Obstetrics and Gynecology. This young doctor, in that first night, taught me how to place IV lines, how to check for labor, and - just after three in the morning - how to deliver a baby.

I was not prepared for the screaming that echoed through the halls of Labor and Delivery. It's one thing to study the anatomy and physiology of pregnancy and childbirth in the quiet of a library. It's quite another to witness the cries of a woman in agony as she pushes a human being out of her body. I watched the baby's head enlarge the opening with each contraction. The young mother-to-be cried and writhed on the delivery table. Blood and body fluids gushed out each time she pushed. Those little details hadn't been mentioned in my textbooks.

I felt sick to my stomach.

The baby's head finally emerged, and the Intern guided my hands to correctly maneuver the baby as she was thrust from the dark warmth of her mother's body. Clutching the tiny newborn to my chest, I watched the Intern cut the cord, and I was suddenly overwhelmed by sublime emotion. There at my first delivery, before I could even put down the baby, I understood that I would dedicate my career to the care of women: I had discovered my purpose in life.

No one was more surprised than I.

As an OB-GYN, I've cared for thousands of women over the past twenty years. I've been married to one woman for twenty-five. As a physician, I'm graced daily with the stories of women. Sometimes single moms soldiering through long work days, coming home to care for children alone at night, long after the fathers are gone. Sometimes older women, struggling to be good mothers and daughters and wives, when they are tired and have nothing left to give.

As a husband, I've watched my wife perform the thankless tasks that mark the seasons of motherhood – the years of changing diapers, the anxious nights awake caring for a sick child, the endless rides and school projects, and the final letting go as they grow up.

Physicians receive an embarrassing quantity of gratitude and respect from their patients. Many have expressed the thought that since I so well understand the difficulties of womanhood, I must be one amazing husband.

I want to say, "Guilty as charged."

Unfortunately for Ann, I am still a guy. By our nature we men approach marriage and life differently. Women think first about the needs of others. We men – at least many of us - tend to think first about ourselves. It's sort of pathetic, really.

In the big picture, the purpose of our lives is to grow spiritually, to focus less on ourselves and more on daily acts of love. Women are hard-wired to love in this capacity; they have a spiritual head start. We men have more growing up to do. This is why marriage is so often critical to a man's spiritual journey. Through faithfulness to a wife and family, we share in the labors of marriage and raising children and become centered on others rather than ourselves. I have been blessed with many male mentors in my medical career. But it is perhaps women – literally, thousands of patients - who have been my most important teachers, not simply in my profession, but more importantly, on the path toward becoming a spiritual grown-up.

The title of Ann's and my book is "Family – A Mismatch Made In Heaven."

For me, the point is this: marriage and family life were conceived in heaven but are lived here on earth.

As we journey together, we face many difficulties that are inherent in biological life. Yet when we understand that our path begins and ends with God, we will see that our struggles are simply signposts along the road –

In the end, helping us find our way back Home.

Acknowledgements

Ann

I am grateful for

My lifelong collaborators - my mother, Elizabeth Wallace, for her numerous insightful suggestions, and my sister Jane Wallace Houlihan, an imaginative sounding board on countless details large and small. My sons, Tyler and Joseph, critics on matters of humor, style, and substance. I am thankful for the contributions of them all.

Criss Farmer for her guidance and wisdom, Bette Cotter for her sunny encouragement, and Jennifer Snyder for her ongoing prayers. My sister-in-law, Suzanne, for her boundless energy, her help and enthusiasm. My father, Joe Wallace, most especially, who taught my sisters and me that we could do whatever we set out to.

Loyal friends and generous teachers, some now gone, who have shaped this work by shaping me. From the University of Michigan, professors Sister Barbara Cervenka and Charles Dwyer of the School of Art and Design. Dr. James Winn, professor of literature, and scholar and teacher of the humanities, who saw in this art student the beginnings of a writer. I continue to strive to do them all justice.

My fellow creative spirits and dreamers, who have seen me through the various stages of my life. They have ventured with me into uncharted territory to build beautiful castles, whether in the art of business, or in the business of art: Tracy Hurh Prescott, Nan Davis, Shawn McLeod, and my brother-in-law Chris.

Our reviewers, beginning with Dr. Johnny Hunt of First Baptist Woodstock, who finds time to not only lead his flock of 15,000, but also assist others throughout the community. Rev. Floyd Tenney and Rev. Lynda Bates-Stepe for their encouragement, along with editors Kara Kiefer, and Brian and Michelle Meeks. Cindy O'Leary and Sonia Carruthers for their inspirational leadership at The Hope Center and Cherokee Focus, respectively.

The community of people in which Michael and I have been blessed to raise our family, where so many work for common good. Thank you for your friendship, for making this corner of the world a uniquely wonderful place.

My sisters Julie and Liza, for their caring empathy and homemade scones. My family - cousins, aunts and uncles, who lend their prayers and support. And my grandfather, the late Reverend Donald Weiglein, who surely continues to watch over us all.

Michael, my life partner and soul mate, keeps me on course as an artist and helped me find my voice as a storyteller. He understands me very well.

Mike

I wish to acknowledge the many mentors who have blessed my life. I will name just a few.

To those who have passed.
Cullen Richardson, MD, Hugh Randall, MD, John Stone, MD, Maria Komaromy, and Mr. Paul Taylor, a Physician Assistant who taught doctors for decades at Grady Memorial Hospital.

To those I don't see much anymore.
William Saye, MD, Sally Nielsen Aversano, H. Kenneth Walker, MD, Young Ahn, MD, Nathan Mordel, MD, Ira Horowitz, MD, Cyril Spann, MD, Sensei Richard Baum, Sensei Al Reingold, and Rita Gulati Kwon, MD.

To those who still cross my path.
James Cross, MD, Vincent Molinari, MD, Joseph Boveri, MD, Brian Raybon, MD, Rev. Floyd Tenney, Dr. Karl Duff, Marilyn Meyer Cramer, and Criss Farmer.

I ask for God's guidance in using the knowledge learned from all my mentors to help alleviate suffering to the best of my ability.

About the Authors

Mike Litrel, MD

is a surgeon, a specialist in women's health care and pelvic reconstructive surgery. He has served as Chief of Surgery and Director of Gynecological Surgery for Atlanta and Houston hospitals respectively, and has held positions on the clinical faculty of both the Emory University School of Medicine and the Medical College of GA.

Dr. Litrel is the author of *The Eyes Don't See*, a book about the relationship between faith and health. He is a speaker for medical conferences and layman audiences, addressing topics related to women's health – relationships, faith and family, and the impact they have on the health of the body. As a Christian physician and a student of world religions, Dr. Litrel brings a balanced perspective to the art of practicing medicine and to his popular writings. His award-winning columns appear in numerous monthly publications. For books and more information, visit mikelitrelmd.com

Ann Litrel

is an artist whose work has appeared on stationery, books, and prints for clients nationwide. She has a studio loft in Woodstock, Georgia, where she creates paintings of historic landmarks, landscapes, and nature, found in corporate and private collections. In 2013, Mrs. Litrel's paintings were chosen to show at the U.S. capital by U.S. Representative Phil Gingrey, representing his congressional district in Atlanta and north Georgia.

Mrs. Litrel has written and illustrated editorial columns on subjects ranging from history to ecology and serves as editor for Dr. Litrel's books and articles. For paintings, writing, and more information, visit annlitrel.com

Photo by Jennifer Carter

Mike and Ann Litrel live in Woodstock, Georgia, with their sons, Tyler and Joseph. Joseph attends public high school, and Tyler is a computer science major at the Georgia Institute of Technology.